460

City Centre

International Opportunities: A Career Guide for Students

International Opportunities: A Career Guide for Students

**A production of
the David M. Kennedy
Center for International Studies**

LIBRARY OF CONGRESS CATALOGING-IN-PUBLICATION DATA

International opportunities: a career guide for students / a production of the David M. Kennedy Center for International Studies

128 p.

1. Employment in foreign countries—Handbooks, manuals, etc. 2. Employment in foreign countries—Vocational guidance. 3. Employment in foreign countries—Directories. 4. Americans—Employment—Foreign countries. I. David M. Kennedy Center for International Studies.

HF5549.5.E45I58 1993
331.7'02—dc20   93–44288
                                                                        CIP

David M. Kennedy Center for International Studies, Brigham Young University
© 1993 by Brigham Young University. All rights reserved
Printed in the United States of America

Distributed by Kennedy Center Publications, Brigham Young University,
PO Box 24538, Provo, Utah 84602–4538; phone (800) 528–6279; fax (801) 378–7075.

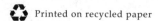 Printed on recycled paper

CONTENTS IN BRIEF

Contents

Preface

How to Get the Most Out of This Guide

Preface
How to Get the Most Out of This Guide

Some of you will automatically skip the preliminary section, race right to the internships, and start sending out resumes. *Please resist the temptation.*

Students looking for a career often assume there is one right career and one right way to find it. While for some, the choice is quickly made (or may even made for them by parents), for others it is a long, at times frustrating and agonizing search.

Finding a career is not a five-minute choice; it's a process. Many people actually stumble into their careers, careers they may not even have known existed. This guide is not meant to help you discover the one perfect job, but it will help you prepare for the right opportunities. Besides, even if you did find the perfect job, you might not find it so perfect after five or ten years.

Even though the information in this guide is specifically oriented toward those interested in working in an international setting, the first section is designed to help you identify activities you enjoy and may indicate potential job markets for you.

You may already know, for example, that you want to teach English abroad. Rather than turning immediately to the teaching section at the end of this guide, take the time to work through the questions in the first section. Ask yourself what aspects of teaching you like best—literature, writing, grammar, English as a second language, etc. Next, ask yourself who you want to teach—Japanese businessmen and women, grade school children, adolescents, "at-risk" children, or young people?

In our experience, students want to know *where* to go to get a job. To give students what they wanted, the original *Guide to International Careers and Opportunities* listed potential employers that students interested in international careers could contact. However, while this approach was easy, it really wasn't useful to most graduates because international organizations generally don't offer entry-level international positions.

Since a single job opening may invite hundreds of applicants, you need to be ready before you approach a potential employer. The revised *International Opportunities: A Career Guide for Students* is intended to guide you through general steps of preparation rather than simply give information on specific international employment opportunities.

As part of your general preparation, this guide begins with several exercises to help you understand your interests and goals in order to choose a course of study. Only when you know "what makes you tick" and what you have to offer will you be ready to zero in on a particular field or type of career.

After the initial exercises, specific information is given to help you choose summer and extra-curricular activities that will help provide the broad experience needed to gain international employment. Also included are various educational organizations and programs that will assist you in gaining language expertise and work experience.

Please note that we do not offer our endorsement to the employers and organizations listed over those not listed. Our intent is only to give students guidelines for career preparation along with a broad sampling of possible opportunities.

We have also listed a broad range of guides and career books. Take time to review some of these resources. This guide is meant primarily to supplement more extensive materials rather than to stand as the only career guide you will ever need.

NOTE: Addresses and phone numbers are given where available, but be aware that they are subject to change.

Part I

Preparing for International Employment

Section 1
Three Steps for the International Job Seeker

Step One: Determine What You Know About Yourself

1. What Makes You Tick?

Some people are motivated by service, others by profit, still others by adventure and variety. If money matters to you, the nonprofit/volunteer sector probably won't offer enough. However, if you're motivated by service and want to "make a difference," it may be just the thing. On the other hand, you may be unhappy in a business that operates on the principle of making a profit. A desk job may drive adventuresome types stir-crazy.

As you plan for some type of international work, examine the career you envision for yourself. You may see yourself in embassies helping Americans. Or you may prefer to use your language experiences with the nationals of a particular country, helping them set up independent businesses. Or you may even be happiest working in the United States with immigrants and international visitors. Consider first where and with whom you wish to work—

In the U.S.	or	Abroad
With Americans		With Americans
With immigrants		With nationals

But wait! some of you may say. What if you don't even know yet what you want, although, you think you'd enjoy traveling, meeting new people, and enjoying diverse cultures. This section is for you too. The exercises that follow ask you to take some time to examine past activities in your life that you have enjoyed, or even disliked, and to plan for future activities that will allow you to grow and use your talents and abilities, while at the same time making a living.

Ask yourself the following questions, placing a 1, 2, or 3 on the line next to the corresponding question.

3

How important is...   Very (3)   Not Very (2)   Not At All (1)

____   • helping others/improving the world?

____   • influencing people/changing others' attitudes
and opinions?

____   • having power/authority to control the work
activities of others?

____   • being directly responsible for the work done by others?

____   • gaining knowledge/seeking truth, wisdom, understanding?

____   • studying/appreciating beautiful things (art,
architecture, etc.)?

____   • making decisions/having power to make decisions?

____   • being recognized for your work in a visible or public way?

____   • being recognized for your expertise or intelligence?

____   • creating new ideas, programs, or products?

____   • having a high degree of excitement or risk-taking in your
work?

____   • exerting yourself in a physically demanding job?

____   • working independently from control of superiors?

____   • having time to spend with your family or pursuing personal
interests?

____   • material gain or money?

The trick is to match up your interests and abilities with the right job market for you. So, if spending time with family has top priority, you know you don't want a high-profile, demanding, eighty-hour-a-week job. If you enjoy variety, risk taking, responsibility, and adventure, you want to watch for work opportunities that allow for more challenge than a routine paper-work job.

These brief exercises won't tell you everything you want to know, but they are a beginning. One of the most important things you can do is take the time to find out what you enjoy—think about your life and those things that you have enjoyed doing and do well. What are you often complemented on? Ask people who know you well what they think you would be happy doing. If you are married, what does your spouse want you to do?

One useful indicator for learning about yourself is an interest/ aptitude test. There are several available, depending on where you go to take the test—a local job service, college counseling or placement center, or employment specialist. You can also use sample tests in books, such as *Do You Understand Me?* by David Keirsey (Del Mar, CA: Prometheus Nemesis, 1984).

Two tests often used in job counseling centers are the *Strong Interest Inventory*, which measures interest in a variety of activities and professions, and the *Myers-Briggs Temperament Test*, which measures extroversion-introversion, judgment-perception, intuition-sensory, thinking-feeling.

Employment specialists are trained to help people make a good career match. Some agencies offer vocational testing, although it is not usually free. Watch out for employment agencies that offer international employment opportunities for an up-front fee. Not only do many cost a great deal, they rarely do anything that you could not do for yourself with a little effort.

2. How Do You Like to Spend Your Time?

Because you change as you grow older, the answer to this question will change from year to year. For this reason, many people often change jobs seven to ten times in a lifetime. This means the job search is often more difficult than the job itself.

The questions below are designed to help you pinpoint certain aspects about yourself that act as indicators of the kind of work environment you may find most satisfying. Take the time to write down your answers, to organize your thoughts and feelings. For example, if you were most unhappy when you went away to school and didn't know anybody, then you may be happiest in a small company where everyone knows each other. You may find a large organization too impersonal.

These questions won't give you the ONE right answer to help you find a career or a major. But as you look at your responses, you should be able to narrow your areas of interest and eliminate areas you aren't interested in.

For instance, if the accomplishment you were proudest of is the story you wrote for the high school newspaper and you enjoy meeting people, you might be happy in journalism. If you are happiest in a rural setting, you may not enjoy Washington, D.C. Don't forget to consider your favorite activities. If they are outdoor events, especially surfing, you may feel tied down at a desk job, particularly in an inland country like Germany.

Knowing what you don't want is also useful. If you worked in a credit union and hated rejecting loan applications, that may also mean you have a soft heart and would feel the same about turning down visa applications if you worked in a foreign embassy.

These brief questions should give you an idea of activities that are satisfying and important to you—at least at this stage of your life. As you begin the job search process, examine employers to see if they allow you the variety, the time for your family, the opportunity to feel you are making a difference, or whatever is important to you.

1. How would you describe yourself to another person? (i.e., tactful, personable, task-oriented, good with numbers or ideas, etc.)

2. What makes you happy? What have you done in the past that has made you happy?

3. What times of your life were you most unhappy? Why?

4. What classes did you (or do you) find most enjoyable and exciting?

5. What kind(s) of work would you like to do? Why would you like to do it?

6. Where would you like to live? City or small town, or in a fairly rural area? What kind of people do you prefer to work with?

7. What marketable skills do you offer an employer?

8. What life accomplishments or honors do you feel proudest of?

9. Do you work better with specific or repetitive work assignments or with more flexibility?

10. What **don't** you want in a job? In a work environment?

Special considerations for those interested in international employment

As you prepare for a career overseas, you may need to match certain interests against each other to choose which to keep. For example, you may never have missed a Super Bowl Sunday in your life, but if your company wants to send you to China to install computers, you may have to miss a few games (or have friends videotape them for you). Or, you may need to forgo those family skiing trips because you'll be doing development work in Niger. No, an international career doesn't require you to give up all your hobbies forever, but your leisure activities may change along with your location.

So in the excitement of accepting a position overseas, remember to consider possible changes in your personal leisure time, as well as other aspects of life—such as your privacy and personal space, your advancement and professional training, and your preferences concerning stability and relocation. Be prepared for extra expenses and major lifestyle changes as well as cultural adaptations.

One of the most important aspects of international living relates to your family. International careers place great demands on the nuclear and extended family, and the family can greatly influence the success of a career. (See the *Infogram* "The International Family," published by the David M. Kennedy Center for International Studies). You will want to consider your spouse's opportunities for employment and social interaction, as well as the educational, social, and cultural opportunities for your children. Married or single, you will want to consider cultural and social opportunities for yourself and your family.

Since many aspects of international living may tend to be glamorized or even overlooked, take time to consider how your life will be changed by living overseas. In addition to the above, a particular concern for international employees is available health services. Do you have diabetes, a heart condition, asthma, etc. Some climates aggravate health conditions more than others, while some health problems requiring constant, reliable, medical care may make an international career unwise.

Step Two: Determine What You Have to Offer

1. What Do You Do Well?

Imagine that you are sitting across the desk from the personnel manager of a large organization. Your resume is on the desk in front of her as she asks, "Why should I hire you?" What are you going to answer?

Well, of course, your answer depends on the job you are applying for, so you can't answer since you don't have enough information. But you can start collecting information right now so, when the time comes, you can give a stunning response.

In fact, you already have one answer from the previous page—the accomplishment you feel most proud of. Maybe you were student body president, so you're a natural leader. Or you worked as a reading tutor, which means you enjoy teaching, motivating, and helping individuals succeed.

Accomplishments

To begin, use the space below to write a list of your accomplishments in various aspects of your life. For example: financial (you paid your way through college) and social (as a teenager you were activities chair of your local youth group). Other aspects include physical, mental, spiritual, vocational, recreational. Consider both your natural aptitudes and developed skills that allowed for these accomplishments.

_____

_____

_____

_____

_____

_____

Skills and Abilities

List your skills next. Can you fix anything with your hands? Are you good with people, tactful with a broad range of people from different cultures, a natural with languages? Remember that not all talents and abilities are obviously visible, like playing a musical instrument or speaking a language. Do you work well independently, without supervision? Are you calm and logical in a crisis? These are all skills.

_____

_____

_____

_____

_____

2. What Skills Do International Employers Look For?

While job requirements vary from position to position, the following skills are often highly valued by employers, so work to develop them through coursework and personal attention during your college years:

- a grasp of past and present trends in international affairs
- a solid understanding of economics and international business transactions
- a knowledge of the public-policy process and how it relates to international affairs
- a firm grounding in the political, social, and economic structure of your own country
- effective speaking and writing skills in your own and other languages
- clear and logical thinking, including sound decision-making skills
- the ability to see cause and effect relationships, particularly in policy implementations
- personal qualities such as poise, humor, open-mindedness, wise judgement, and intellectual curiosity

Generally, a B.A. in international studies will not provide adequate preparation for most international careers. Many international positions dealing with foreign affairs require expertise in other fields, such as finance, business management, engineering, or law. Other international positions require advanced degrees and extensive international experience. Since getting a degree does not always mean getting an education, remember to focus your courses in areas that will be sought by employers.

A college graduate with a B.A. in international relations, political science, English, Spanish, or history may be disadvantaged in the competitive job world unless they can combine their advanced degree with experience. For this reason, you may want to consider a double major, an advanced degree, or even multiple internships to gain experience. (Just taking a few business-related courses will not suffice, as business employers usually seek candidates with degrees in some business-related field).

Other examples of valuable combinations with international or area studies degrees include accounting, agriculture, business administration, computer science, economics, engineering, food science and nutrition, foreign languages, geology, journalism, international business, liberal arts, and marketing.

3. How Can You Best Represent Yourself On Your Resume?

If you don't yet have a resume, begin it immediately, even if you aren't looking for a job. You never know when an opportunity to use it will arise, so update it about every six months.

Remember, too, that most employers give the average resume thirty seconds. Each word needs to count, and your format must be absolutely readable.

Numerous resume guides can be found in every library, and many resume services are available. Watch for resume and interviewing workshops, which are often offered by placement or career counseling offices at local colleges. Visit with career counselors.

Resumes are normally kept to two pages; many recommend one page only. As you gain experience, a resume for an international position may require more length. However, the most pertinent and important information should be on the first two pages. Some recommend a "summary" on the first page so the most important information is accessible.

If you've done the exercises at the beginning of this section, you should have a list of your skills, accomplishments, and interests. This will help you more easily identify your *accomplishments* and *contributions* rather than your responsibilities at various jobs. For instance, employers are more impressed by the statement "created an accessible filing system that increased employee productivity" than by simply "responsible for accessing and filing information."

Resumes should be done on a word processor rather than type-writer. Use quality bond paper rather than erasable paper. White is always acceptable, although other subtle colors, such as tan and gray will help set your resume apart. Use laser quality printing rather than dot matrix. Remember to give your resume adequate margins on all sides.

After you have written your resume, be sure to tailor it for each job. Stress the particular abilities and experience you've had that directly relate to the position you are interested in. If education is the most important qualification, list it first. If experience is most important, list it first. In applying for an international position, emphasize your international experience and skills that are transferrable to an international setting.

Caution: If a resume service creates your resume, be sure to proof it carefully. Make sure it says what you want it to say. Don't leave all the responsibility to the people who prepare it; they even make mistakes.

Step Three: Start to Gain Experience NOW

1. What Can You Do Now If You Are a Student in the United States?

First, regardless of where you want to work or what you want to do, you can still be doing things *right now* that can make a difference in your future.

Increase your marketability

Take every opportunity to learn to communicate verbally and in writing. Many employers bemoan the inability of their employees to write. Attend tutor sessions or writing labs if necessary. Begin your assignments early and revise your writing to make it better. Many recommend *Elements of Style* (William Strunk and E. B. White), *Style: Ten Lessons in Clarity and Grace* (Joseph M. Williams), and *Writing with Style* (John Trimble) as helpful guides.

Study a second or third language. Knowing another language may not get you the job (unless it's as a translator or interpreter), but it may get you the promotion after you get the job.

Make time in your class schedule to go beyond the life of the student. Watch for workshops and seminars. Learn sign language, karate, typing, computers, technical writing.

Make your schooling work for you

Get the best grades you can and gain the respect of your instructors by getting to class on time, being interested, and doing your best work.

Make an appointment with a teacher you admire and ask how they decided on their profession. Ask what they would do differently. They'll appreciate your interest in them, and they may just pass on a tip or two that made the difference. Or, maybe you'll feel comforted knowing how long and circuitous—or surprising—the route has been for others.

Establish good relationships with professors who are in a position to write you letters of recommendation. Keep your papers or assignments for their classes with their written comments in a folder. When you ask professors to write letters, they can refresh their memories of your skills by looking through the folder of your work and rereading their comments.

Go beyond your classwork

Participate in domestic volunteer opportunities while you are in school. Not everyone can give two years to the Peace Corps, but opportunities abound for volunteers. Wherever you live, libraries need volunteers to take books to the elderly. Public schools usually need aides or tutors. Your local newspaper may list volunteer services. Check your telephone book under Volunteer or Community Services in the city or county government sections. The Points of Light Foundation at (800) 879-5400 can provide the phone number of a volunteer center near you, and additional information on volunteering.

At least every two years, you will have opportunities to assist in campaigning for a local or national political candidate. Being formally involved will give you valuable experience and open doors that may lead to international work.

Participate in clubs and professional societies. Join a language club or an international association in your field of interest. Write for a newsletter, give presentations, volunteer to help organize an annual symposium.

Publish your work. Most universities have a variety of student journals in different academic areas —literary and international studies are just two examples. Most employers value proven experience and skill in writing and publishing.

2. How Can You Gain Good International Experience?

Even with a heavy class schedule and a determination to get straight As, you can add a few things to your life that will give you experience working with different varieties of people. Instead of an evening in front of the TV, spend a few hours on a service project—the local shelter or the Special Olympics. Join an international student outreach program or offer to teach citizenship or job skills classes to immigrants. You will gain experience with people, knowledge of yourself, and relationships with people willing to serve as references— all of which will help you in your pursuit of an international career. Additional ideas for involvement are listed below and in the resource list at the end of this section.

Many **internship** opportunities are available to both undergraduate and graduate students during summers or during the school year, concurrently with classes. While international internships are more difficult to obtain, a domestic internship serves many of the same purposes in allowing you to explore your interests and develop your knowledge and skills by integrating theory and experience. Many international organizations have domestic offices that accept interns, helping you to develop cross-cultural communication skills, clarify your career goals, and increase your self-confidence.

Many organizations have **student exchange programs** that promote educational and cultural exchange for high school and college students. Students live with a host family rather than in a dormitory as they may in study abroad programs. (See the resource list for the names and addresses of some of these organizations.)

Most **study abroad** programs have a general education emphasis, including humanities, social science, language training, and history, although a few contain a practical internship component as well. Both types of programs provide opportunities that are unavailable at home. First, these programs will get you into other countries. They give you important exposure to other cultures, so you can make sure that you are truly internationally minded, and assure future employers who may wish to send you overseas that you know what you're getting into. An important consideration is that study abroad opportunities are usually much easier to obtain than internships. The presence of classmates and faculty, and the familiarity of an educational environment, usually make a study abroad experience enjoyable and relatively painless.

Travel study goes beyond the ordinary tourist experience, providing one-to four-week tours in many parts of the world. College credit is offered, sometimes at no additional cost. For more information, contact the travel study office at a nearby university or the Council on International Educational Exchange, which publishes information on various travel study programs.

Work abroad programs are offered by Council on International Educational Exchange, allowing students to work abroad legally on a temporary basis. CIEE has agreements with the governments of Canada, Costa Rica, France, Germany, Ireland, Jamaica, New Zealand, the United Kingdom, and the United States to allow U.S. students to work in those countries, as well as to allow students from those countries to work in the United States. In 1990, more than six thousand students from over one thousand U.S. colleges and universities traveled overseas and, on average, found some type of employment within three days of arrival. CIEE is not an employment agency, but its cooperating organizations provide job listings, orientations, and various handbooks.

International **work camps** were instituted after World War I to help rebuild war-torn Europe. Since then, similar programs have been established throughout most of the developing world as a form of short-term voluntary service in which a small group of people live together and work on a common project. The most common work program since the 1960s has been the **Peace Corps**, which operates under the auspices of the U.S. government to promote American understanding of and appreciation for cultures in developing nations, to allow those peoples to better appreciate Americans, and to allow Americans to serve and gain experience in the development field. **CIEE** also offers summer international work-camp experience. Project length varies from three weeks to two years. Benefits also vary but can include such things as free room and board, transportation within the country, travel-cost reimbursement, insurance, and pocket money. Projects are generally in areas such as agriculture, construction, welfare work, environmental protection, and work study. **Volunteers for Peace (VFP)** is another international work-camp program with eight hundred programs in over forty countries. It provides short-term opportunities to work abroad.

Last but not least, look for and take opportunities to travel on your own or with a group. Even travel within the United States can be beneficial. Although, as a student you may not have a great deal of discretionary income, consider your travel a necessary investment in your future to establish experience and marketability. Watch for student discounts.

3. Where Can Students Go to Get International Exposure?

The organizations listed below provide various services and information for students seeking an international study or work experience (see also the resources listed at the end of this section):

American Institute for Foreign Study
102 Greenwich Avenue
Greenwich, CT 06830
(800) 727-2437
(203) 869-9090

Institute for International Development and Cooperation (IIDC)
PO Box 103-P
Williamstown, MA 01267
(413) 458-9828

Volunteers study a particular region and its language, gain practical training, participate in fundraising, then work on projects in Africa or Latin America. They return home to give public presentations and produce educational materials.

Rotary International
The Rotary Foundation
One Rotary Center
1560 Sherman Avenue
Evanston, IL 60201
(708) 866-3000
Scholarship assistance.

School for International Living
Experiment in International Living
Kipling Road
PO Box 676
Brattleboro, VT 05302-0676
(800) 451-4465 ext. 29

Student Conservation Association
PO Box 550
Charlestown, NH 03603
(603) 543-1700
Students work in wildlife refuge areas.

YMCA International Camp Counselor Program
356 West 34th Street
New York, NY 10001
(212) 727-8800
Counselors need previous YMCA work experience.

SECTION 2
BEWARE OF MYTHS ABOUT INTERNATIONAL WORK

Myth 1: *I'll land a job in Vienna with IBM, travel all over Europe, and meet lots of interesting people.*

Many international jobs actually involve very little travel. You might work in one location, perhaps an extremely isolated spot, for the entire duration of your assignment, with neither the time nor income to do more travel. Some international jobs are based in the United States, requiring only occasional travel abroad. Many federal employees spend much of their career in Washington, D.C. For those with international positions, the only travel they may ever experience is to and from their job site abroad.

Myth 2: *An international job is glamorous and exciting.*

Some jobs are exciting, some are boring. Much of the excitement comes from learning about different cultures and lifestyles, and meeting new people. Not all places are glamorous; some are remote, even dangerous, with few luxuries such as a microwave, TV, VCR, etc. You may also be without running water or good local health care. Some international positions may involve health risks incurred by a poor water supply or high pollution levels. The only thing you can count on for sure is that things will be different from what you are used to.

Myth 3: *I'll start sending my resume as soon as I graduate and have the time. Then I'll have a "real" job and a "real" salary in no time.*

College students are finding that even with a degree, it may take several months out of college to find a good job. One job opening may attract hundreds of applications. To make your job search less stressful, prepare now—send out resumes early, ask friends and colleagues about their work, and build up a nest egg to support you through a few months of not working.

International work may be even more challenging to find, as most companies do not have entry level jobs for international positions. Oftimes, only those employees who have been with the company and have proven their worth and expertise are entrusted with the international positions. Be prepared to begin with a domestic position and work on gaining competency and skill in your field.

Myth 4: An 8–5 job will leave me with my weekends and Saturdays free.

Some jobs, particularly at the beginning, will expect long evenings and, yes, even weekends.

Myth 5: Since international work pays so well, with my cost of living allowance, I'll be making big bucks in no time.

Some jobs may pay very well, others quite poorly. Often international living incurs unique expenses as well as lost income (i.e., job opportunities for one's spouse). Work with the government or non-profit organizations probably won't make you wealthy. The best reasons for working abroad are a love of the world and its different cultures and peoples and the desire to use your abilities to make the world a better place.

Myth 6: English is the international language, and since I'll be working with other Americans, it won't matter if I speak another language or not.

No, it isn't always necessary to speak a second language to work overseas. But, you never know the opportunities you may miss by not speaking at least one additional language. The government foreign service doesn't require foreign language proficiency of its new recruits; however, it *is* required in order to advance. You will also find examples of international businessmen and women who have survived without learning the language of the country they work and live in, but they may often wish they knew the language.

Myth 7: I'll find work in a developing country where I can really make a difference in the world.

Work in developing countries is important but it can also be frustrating. The process of change can be very slow. Some people don't want to change. People working to improve conditions in developing countries will find that it is not realistic to expect that one person can enter a well established culture and change ideas, feelings, goals, patterns of thinking, or mindsets in a few years.

Myth 8: *With my two years of teaching experience in Japan and my three weeks at a work camp in Spain when I was in high school, I shouldn't have any trouble convincing an employer that I'm international material.*

True—you've shown that you've had some international exposure and perhaps adapt to different cultures well. But two years of, say, teaching English classes, or three weeks digging ditches won't convince an employer that you're ready for the world of international finance.

What will help, in addition to your international experience, may be your volunteer work as a budget officer for your local food bank or as a financial counselor in a community consumer credit organization. This may open the way to an internship with a larger nonprofit organization or government financial institution such as the World Bank.

Myth 9: *My friends have a great living allowance and live in a palace. Everything is paid for by their company.*

Wouldn't it be nice? Living allowances and housing will vary according to the location and the company you work for. Seniority also plays a role in the kind of housing you will get. If you are lucky enough to live in a palace, enjoy it by all means. But be prepared for the greater likelihood of a regular apartment. You may also find greater privations (for example, no phone or car) than luxuries.

Myth 10: *Once I've established myself as a capable international employee, there's no place to go but up. And if I decide at some point to go back to the United States, my experience should get me a good promotion and a raise.*

Some people returning from work abroad may find that they no longer fit into old positions and their highly specialized work has not qualified them for new positions. In addition, you will have other personal and familial adjustments to make. (See the *Infogram* "Coming Home Again," published by the David M. Kennedy Center for International Studies.)

Myth 11: *Sure, my spouse and kids will have some adjusting to do, but once we're all moved in, they'll love it.*

They may, and they may not. Adjustment is a very personal matter. International careers place great demands on the nuclear and extended family. Although some people underestimate the challenges of an international career for a family, some families find an international experience unifying. Cultural and linguistic barriers often bring family members closer together. On the other hand, living abroad can be stressful and uncomfortable for some. A great deal of sacrifice and flexibility are necessary for a valuable international experience. Sometimes family members find this impossible. A family's particular circumstances and attitudes can significantly affect the success of one's international career.

You can help your spouse and children prepare for an international experience by studying the country and language together, and by working out questions and problems in advance. Discuss your expectations, the benefits they can look forward to, and the sacrifices they may be expected to make. Remember, most companies aren't impressed when their international employees request a transfer home after only a few months abroad. (For more information, see the *Infogram* "The International Family," published by the David M. Kennedy Center for International Studies.)

Section 3
Resources for Students

If books are not available at a local library or university placement office, they can be ordered from the publisher. A complete resource list is given at the end of the guide.

Organizations

AFS Intercultural Programs, 220 East 42d Street, 3d floor, New York, NY 10017. (800) AFS-INFO or (212) 949-4242 ext. 538.

Council on International Educational Exchange (CIEE), 205 East 42d Street, New York, NY 10017. (212) 661-1414.

International Christian Youth Exchange, 134 West 26th Street, New York, NY 10001. (212) 206-7307.

Institute of International Education (IEE), 809 UN Plaza, New York, NY 10017. (212) 883-8200.

National Association for Foreign Student Affairs (NAFSA), 1875 Connecticut Avenue, NW, Suite 1000, Washington, DC 20009. (202) 462-4811.

Volunteers for Peace (VFP), 43 Tiffany Road, Belmont, VT 04730. (802) 259-2759.

Newsletters

Transitions Abroad: The Guide to Learning, Living, and Working Overseas (1 yr./6 issues, $18). *Transitions Abroad*, Department TRA, PO Box 3000, Denville, NJ 07834. Offers information on overseas employment, study, and travel, listing additional information and materials, as well as specific names and addresses of people and organizations to contact.

Publications

Basic Facts on Foreign Study 1990-91. CIEE. 205 East 42d Street, New York, NY 10017. (212) 661-1414.

"Foreign Visa Requirements." Consumer Information Center, Department 438T, Pueblo CO 81009. Publication no. 9517.

The International Family. David M. Kennedy Center for International Studies, Brigham Young University, Provo, Utah 84602-4538. (800) 528–6279.

International Work Camps. CIEE. 205 East 42d Street, New York, NY 10017. (212) 661-1414.

Learning Vacations. 1989. 6th ed. Gerson G. Eisenberg. Peterson's Guides. (800) EDU-DATA.

1993 International Workcamps Directory and *The International Workcamper*, the Annual Newsletter of VFP International Workcamps. For a $10-100 contribution, you will receive these publications. Send check to VFP, 43 Tiffany Road, Belmont, VT 04730. (802) 259-2759.

"A Safe Trip Abroad." US Government Printing Office, Washington, DC 20402. ($1)

Student Travel Catalog 1991. CIEE. (212) 661-1414.

Work Abroad. CIEE. (212) 661-1414.

Work, Study, Travel Abroad: The Whole World Handbook, 1992-93. 11th ed. CIEE. Available from St. Martin's Press, 175 Fifth Avenue, New York, NY 10010. (800) 221-7945.

"Your Trip Abroad." US Government Printing Office, Washington, DC 20402 ($1).

Part II

Internships

SECTION 4
IS AN INTERNSHIP FOR YOU?

Some people, after a brief visit to another country, may feel international life is for them. Others may have lived in another country temporarily, as an exchange student for example, and long to return as a teacher. Before accepting a full-time, permanent teaching position there, however, it would be wise to accept a short-term teaching contract to see if life as a resident is as enjoyable as life as a visitor.

An **international internship** will help you gain the experience necessary to find work in a competitive job market. It will also give you a better idea of whether or not an international career really is for you. In addition to offering unique cultural and work experiences, an internship will help you:

- gain a knowledge of procedures

- learn the standards of expected work behavior

- create a network of contacts in the working world

- gain references for future employment

- show potential employers your skills, dependability, and flexibility

- practice and increase your employable skills in a "real" setting

- understand and examine your own abilities, limitations, and goals.

Since a great deal of international work is done in the United States, not all international internships will place you overseas. Nevertheless, a domestic internship will still provide an excellent learning experience. Domestic internships may also be easier to obtain, and at the same time, they serve many of the same purposes. Another important consideration is that a domestic internship may pave the way for a second internship, one overseas this time.

If you are willing to volunteer your time and step out of your "comfort zone," you will find many opportunities to gain experience. Paid internships are less abundant; however, they do exist. Since paid international internships are competitive, you may want to consider unpaid internships as well as other ways to gain experience.

In general, most internships are geared toward college students or even graduate students, but a few are available to high school students. Many specify invitations to international applicants and/or minority students and make note of their accessibility to the handicapped. Some assistance may be given in locating housing. At times, there is the possibility of full-time employment.

Competition is intense and you will want to carefully prepare your resume and cover letter to show that while you are willing and eager to learn, you also have a lot to contribute.

Some Statistics on Internships

Internships are offered through cooperative education programs at most universities and colleges. The "co-op ed" office helps students arrange internships as part of their education with cooperating businesses and organizations. Many internship opportunities are often available with volunteer and nonprofit organizations, large companies, and the government, but you may also find or create internships in a variety of unexpected places.

- An estimated 50,000 employers, both public and private, hire interns as cooperative education students.

- More than 250,000 interns participate in cooperative education programs.

- Approximately 900 colleges and universities, both two and four year, offer cooperative education programs. College credit is usually available.

- Reports taken at universities involved in cooperative education programs show that 80 percent of interns receive an offer for permanent employment from a company that participates in the university's program; 63 percent of the co-op students receive offers from their final co-op employer; and 48 percent of the intern students accept the job offers. (Statistics do not indicate whether internships are domestic or international; however, these statistics likely indicate domestic internships.)

- On average, co-op students earn approximately $7,500 a year, although earnings vary. (Statistics prepared by the National Commission for Cooperative Education.)

Section 5
What's Involved in Getting an Internship?

A good internship may be as competitive as a "real" job, so prepare your application and resume as carefully as you would if you were applying for a job. Some guidelines are listed here to help you apply for an internship. (More information on creating a resume is found on pages 23-24 of this guide. See also the resources listed at the back of this guide.) In addition to your cover letter, resume, and application, internship sponsors may also ask for a writing sample, college transcripts, and two letters of recommendation.

Prepare a **cover letter** to accompany your resume. A cover letter gives you the opportunity to emphasize your strengths and relate them specifically to the organization. It also allows you to explain why you seek this internship and how it will be of benefit to you in your long-range goals. (Remember, you are the "seller," not the "buyer." Most candidates are not in a position to pick and choose; whereas, the hiring agencies have a wide selection of candidates from which to choose.) Be sure to include in your letter how and when you may be contacted for an interview.

An **interview** serves two purposes—to let the internship sponsor know if you are for them, and to let you know if they are for you. You may learn that this internship won't really give you what you're looking for. Since personal interviews are more to your advantage than telephone interviews, you might want to schedule several interviews during a school break. Be prepared to ask questions as well as to answer them. This will help you get the information you need to choose the right internship. The following are only a sample:

Questions You May Ask

1. What were the responsibilities of the last intern/person in this position?

2. What do you consider the most important qualities are in a successful intern or employee?

3. How many hours of overtime are employees usually expected to work?

4. How does this position relate to or impact other positions in the organization?

Questions Employers May Ask

1. Tell me about yourself.

2. Why do you want to work for this company?

3. What is your greatest weakness? Your greatest strength? Your greatest success?

4. Where do you see yourself in the future?

5. Was there anything you didn't like about your last job?

How to Ensure a Successful Internship

Before the Internship

- Plan early to set up an internship. If you put off your internship until your senior year, you may have to choose between practical experience and the one last class required for graduation. An internship during your sophomore or junior year can give you more focus in your class work.

- Be prepared to choose between getting experience and getting paid. Of course, getting paid for the work you do is nice. But, far more important at this stage is gaining experience. If you need to limit your internship to those that pay, you may miss out on some valuable learning.

- Talk to previous interns to learn what they learned. It may save you time and grief.

- Decide in advance what you want to get out of your internship. Keep a journal to evaluate what you learn. (Some cooperative education internships require a daily record or written evaluation of your learning.)

Some internships will require that you write up a **learning contract**. This is a good idea even if you are not assigned to write one. A learning contract will help you define your goals and serves to delineate the expectations of your employer. Your supervisor can help you create your contract, which includes the following:

- your *responsibilities* (What are your day-to-day duties?)

- *learning objectives* (What skills or knowledge do you want to learn through your duties?)

- *criteria for evaluation* (Who will "grade" your work and how will you know that you have met your learning objectives?).

During the Internship

- Discuss your expectations with your supervisor. If you aren't getting the feedback you need, ask your supervisor to take time with you to review your progress.

- Volunteer for extra responsibilities, and remember to thank your supervisors and coworkers for their help.

- Be prepared to learn aspects of the job that you hadn't planned on learning. For instance, you may find that eight hours at a desk isn't for you or that the risk and pressure of high finance leaves you unable to sleep at night. Knowing that your current goals won't really satisfy you allows you to find other career paths that will be more satisfying before you get much further down the wrong road.

After the Internship

- Before the internship ends, have a plan of action for what to do next. If no job offer seems imminent, start your job search early, though not on company time. If you get a job offer but want to return to school, or you find work in a different area, thank your supervisor but explain that you have other plans. In any case, plan ahead so that you aren't sitting home by the phone.

- Send thank-you notes to your supervisor and in some cases, to coworkers who were especially helpful.

What to Do If Your Internship
Isn't the Positive Experience You Expected?

Sometimes, no matter how hard you try, your internship doesn't give you the learning experience you wanted. Your position may be seen merely as "free labor" for a busy company, and you may be assigned the stacks of filing or other menial assignments that nobody wanted. You may get little or no specific directions or feedback on your performance. You may find yourself working for nothing or next to nothing and feel like your internship is a waste of time.

If that happens, make the best of the situation and don't give up. Be pleasant, watch for ways to be efficient and useful. Then look for other internships in your area of interest, using your experience to evaluate the next position to see if it will offer the challenge and learning that your previous internship did not.

Section 6
Where to Find Internships

NOTE: If you skipped section one, go back and look through the exercises. Where you look and what you find often depends, to a great extent, on where you start.

This section contains a brief selection of paid and unpaid internships that are available in the federal government, non-profit, and volunteer organizations.

Specific private sector internships are not listed; rather, various resources are given that will help you locate your own. The resource list at the end of this section suggests publications and directories that give company names and addresses so you can set up an internship directly. (See also the private sector resources in section eight.)

In addition to the list of resources for finding internships at the end of this section, the cooperative education office or international internship office at your university may also be useful. In many cases, internships are offered through the various language departments at colleges and universities.

You may also be able to create your own internship by approaching the company you wish to work for. Various business directories will give you the names and addresses of companies you are interested in. Focus on a few companies and learn about them by researching newspapers, business journals, etc. (Many companies often produce an annual report for stockholders.) Based on your research and your knowledge of your own skills, make an appointment with the supervisor in the department you are interested in to discuss the feasibility of an internship.

Federal Government

Even though interns are not usually placed in overseas locations, don't let that put you off. An office or company with overseas offices will still give you valuable work and international experience. The federal government has many offices with international connections, and is the largest employer of interns, with over 15,000 student interns in 36 federal departments and agencies at almost 2,000 worksites.

Some, but not all, internships may be listed with the hotline for government positions, Career America Connection (912) 757-3000. In general, it's best to contact the individual department or agency to learn about possible internships.

In addition to the individual internships offered by various agencies and departments, the federal government offers several National Student Employment Programs created to attract students to a career in public service while helping to finance their education. Information on these programs can be obtained by calling the Office of Personnel Management at (202) 606-3283/3284.

For High School Students

1. The **Stay in School** program is for students enrolled full time in a high school or vocational/technical school. They must be in need of earnings, and qualify under the financial need criteria based on family income. Some of the stay-in-school fields where students work include administrative and office support, professional and technical trades and crafts, and student aide positions.

   To apply for a stay-in-school position, directly contact the federal agency you wish to work for, or you may apply through your local State Employment Service (SES) Office.

2. **Federal Junior Fellowship Program** is a career-related work/study program that allows students to make money while applying the knowledge they are learning in college. Candidates should be graduating high school seniors with a strong academic record who have been accepted or are planning to attend a baccalaureate or associate degree program. They must demonstrate financial need and qualify under the financial need criteria based on family income. Junior fellows may work in administration, biological sciences, education, public information, or a number of other areas.

   To apply, contact the guidance counselor or teacher at your school who is responsible for the Federal Junior Fellowship Program. You may also contact the personnel office at any federal agency or the U.S. Office of Personnel Management's (OPM) area office nearest you. Your high school guidance counselor or teacher nominates eligible seniors for program consideration.

For College Students

1. The **Federal Cooperative Education Program** is one of the government's leading national student employment programs. Co-op students may fill assignments in a wide array of career-enhancing public service work experiences across the country in laboratories, offices, forests, parks, shipyards, hospitals, and in ocean and space programs. Students may work in accounting, communications, business, engineering, the social sciences, and other fields.

   Co-op students may alternate periods of work and study, or work part time and attend school part time. To be a co-op student, contact your cooperative education office or the Cooperative Education Program Manager in the personnel office of any federal agency. Applicants must be enrolled in their school's cooperative education program and be recommended for a co-op position.

2. The **Summer Aid Program and Summer Employment Program** gives students exposure to the federal work environment as well as early career exploration and experience. Summer employees perform seasonal work and work to ease the impact of the vacation schedules of permanent employees. Employment opportunities range from office support to trade and labor jobs, to professional positions.

   Summer positions are competitive, so apply early (December). You can either call the Career America College Hotline (1-900-990-9200), contact any U.S. Office of Personnel Management area office, or call the Federal Job Information Center and request the government's Summer Jobs Announcement #414. The government also publishes *Summer Job Opportunities*, which can be found at your nearest OPM office or local job information center.

   For Summer Aid positions, which are especially geared for the economically disadvantaged, go to the State Employment Service (SES) Office in your area. This office will verify your financial eligibility and make job referrals. The phone numbers for these offices can be found in the government listing section of your telephone directory under "State Government."

3. The **Volunteer Service Program** provides unpaid, academically related work assignments for high school and college students.

Most student volunteers are involved in professional projects and activities that run the gamut from policy to research oriented tasks, to projects involving wildlife initiatives, environmental concerns, and congressional issues.

Volunteer internships may last three to four months at any time during the year. To become a student volunteer, directly contact the federal agency or department you wish to work for, or visit your school's career counseling, placement, cooperative education, or internship office for more information. You may also wish to consult the *Federal Career Directory*, a reference book that will provide you with descriptions of over 160 federal agencies and departments along with their missions and responsibilities.

Foreign-Oriented Agencies

Note: An asterisk (*) means that this entry is cross referenced with a similar entry in the section on job-seeking. A sample of internships is listed below. For other government internships, check the various publications that list internships (see the resource list at the end of this section).

The **U.S. Agency for International Development (USAID)*** administers the foreign economic assistance programs of the U.S. government with representatives in approximately seventy developing countries throughout the world. The *International Development Intern (IDI)* program is the agency's entry-level program designed to train qualified men and women to become Foreign Service Officers as they assume positions of increasing responsibility in planning, implementing, and managing USAID's economic assistance activities overseas.

Candidates should have a bachelor's or master's degree with two years of work experience. They must be available worldwide to serve two years in the foreign service as USAID Foreign Services Officers. It is expected that Foreign Service Officers will spend the majority of their careers abroad.

Selection for the IDI program is highly competitive. Candidates are evaluated in terms of academic credentials, related overseas and professional domestic experience, and other relevant factors. While language proficiency is not a requirement for hiring, credit for demonstrated language proficiency is given to candidates selected for appointment. If candidates do not speak a foreign language, they will receive training in French or Spanish before going overseas.

Dedication to a career in international development—rather than just an occasional overseas assignment—must be each intern's objective. Maturity, good character, tolerance, sensitivity, and adaptability are essential qualities for working with individuals and organizations that participate in the development process overseas. To apply, send a completed Federal Employment Form (SF-171) to the following address:

Agency for International Development
International Development Intern Program
Recruitment Division
515 22d Street, NW
Washington, DC 20523
(202) 663-1408

The **Department of State*** is the executive branch of the federal government, responsible for administering U.S. foreign policy and for maintaining diplomatic relations throughout the world. Headquartered in Washington, D.C., with more than 230 embassies and consulates abroad, the department covers over 140 countries.

Both paid and unpaid internships are available in various areas: international, human rights, African affairs, inspector general's office, diplomatic security, information management, economic and business, finance and management, intelligence research, personnel, and politico-military. Interns may also work in the Bureaus of Administration, Consular Affairs, International Narcotics Matters, International Organization Affairs, Legislative and Intergovernmental Affairs, Oceans and International Environmental and Scientific Affairs, Public Affairs, Refugee Programs, and International Communications and Information Policy.

Internships are open to juniors, seniors, and graduate students. Applicants should have an academic background in the area for which they are applying. While many positions are located in Washington, D.C., some posts abroad are available. A limited number of paid internships are also available for members of minority groups identified under Title VII of the Civil Rights Acts of 1964 .

Application deadlines are 1 November for summer, 1 March for fall, and 1 July for spring. Most internships require a security check. For information, send a postcard to:

US Department of State
Intern Coordinator
PO Box 9317
Arlington, VA 22219
(703) 875-7490

The **Department of State Office of the Legal Adviser** provides legal advice on all domestic and international legal problems arising in the course of the department's activities. Internships are offered to second-year law students. Work-study internships are available for the fall and spring semesters for second-year students and in the fall for third-year students. Deadlines for the summer internship and the fall work study internship is 1 November. The deadline for the spring work-study internship is 1 March. For these internships, second-year law students applying for summer internships or for the work-study program must submit a resume and copy of law school transcripts. Send applications to:

Executive Director
Office of the Legal Adviser
US Department of State
2201 C Street, NW
Washington, DC 20520-6417
(202) 647-9417

The **Export-Import Bank of the United States (Eximbank)** facilitates export financing of U.S. goods and services by matching the effect of export credit subsidies from other governments and by absorbing reasonable credit risks that are beyond the current reach of the private sector. It also encourages foreign buyers to purchase U.S. exports by offering competitive, fixed-rate loans.

Eximbank offers volunteer spring, summer, and fall internships during which interns assist bank staff in the areas of financial analysis, economics, accounting, information systems management, and administration. Applications are accepted between 1 January and 15 March for the Eximbank Internship Program. Internships are also available through the Presidential Management Internship (PMI) program (see page 46). For more information, contact:

Export-Import Bank of the United States
Attn: Human Resources
Room 1005
811 Vermont Avenue, NW
Washington, DC 20571
(202) 566-8834

The **U.S. Information Agency (USIA)*** is concerned primarily with promoting mutual understanding by providing information about American events and culture to citizens of foreign countries. One of its responsibilities is the **Voice of America (VOA)**,* a radio network that broadcasts news and information in forty-nine languages to most countries of the world.

The **News and English Broadcasts Directorate (NEB)** of VOA employs approximately 250 people who write, produce, and broadcast news, special events, music, Americana, feature, and cultural programming to listeners in all areas of the world. NEB is comprised of the News Division, Current Affairs Division, and Worldwide English Division.

The purpose of the VOA Intern Program is to develop skills of the best qualified candidates for future writing, editorial, and managerial positions in VOA. Interns are trained to work in all phases of NEB: feature and documentary writing, news writing and programming, voicing, production, reporting, etc. Candidates should have a background in broadcast journalism, communications, international relations or area studies, with strong writing skills and broadcasting potential. The program is not for the novice, nor for one without academic background in or practical exposure to the field of broadcast communications.

English Intern positions are filled at the GS-7, step 1 level. Interns are eligible to enroll in both health and life insurance programs available to federal employees. Applications are especially invited from qualified women, minorities, veterans, and the handicapped. For information write:

US Information Agency
Voice of America Personnel Office
301 Fourth Street, SW
Washington, DC 20547
(202) 619-4700

Volunteer interns are also accepted to give students an opportunity for practical work experience and early career exploration. Applicants must be enrolled full or part time in an accredited educational institution. The application deadline for summer is the first week in April, although applications after this date are accepted. To apply, students must complete and send in an SF-171, an IA-14, and a brief (one paragraph) writing sample explaining their long-term career objective(s), relevant work experience they have had, and the way their talents would contribute to Voice of America. The forms and narrative should be mailed to:

Bureau of Broadcasting
Voice of America VOA/POP
Room 1543, Cohen Building
330 Independence Avenue, SW
Washington, DC 20547
(202) 619-3117

Inter-American Foundation (IAF) is a federal agency whose purpose is to support the self-help efforts of poor people in Latin America and the Caribbean. The foundation responds directly to initiatives of the poor by supporting grassroots organizations such as agricultural cooperatives, community associations, and small urban enterprises, as well as larger service organizations that work with local groups, and provide them with credit, technical assistance, training, and marketing services.

The *Student Volunteer Internship Program* offers unpaid semester internships in various offices throughout the organization. *Learning and Dissemination* student volunteers are involved in ongoing research projects on the relationship between non-governmental development organizations (NGO) and local governments in Latin America. Interns review IAF-supported projects, complete bibliographical survey work in the Library of Congress , review manuscripts, and do research and editing. Volunteers in the *Office of Programs* assist with research and analysis of grant proposals.

Volunteer interns should have a background in Latin America, Caribbean, or Third World development issues, financial management, human resource management, law, research, and development. Fluency in French, Haitian Creole, Spanish, or Portuguese is required for some assignments. Applicants must be available to work at least twelve hours per week in increments of at least four hours a day. To apply, complete and send an SF-71 form to the address below or contact:

Inter-American Foundation
Student Volunteer Program
901 North Stuart Street
Arlington, VA 22203
(703) 841-3800

The **Office of the US Trade Representative**, in the Executive Office of the President, offers volunteer internships throughout the year for both graduate and undergraduate students.

Unpaid internships that last from three to twelve months are available for students with backgrounds in business and finance, economics, international relations, area studies, liberal arts, mathematics, statistics, languages, and business or public administration.

Interns generally work with research and writing assignments, report on hearings and meetings, and complete analyses, statistics, and briefings on books. An intern may investigate the impact of changes on a country's political economy, compile data for a report on the discrepancies between U.S. and Taiwan trade statistics, draft economic profiles of various countries, or assist in briefings of interagency delegations that investigate government policies on the procurement of heavy electrical equipment.

Send a resume, writing sample, and cover letter stating period of availability, including number of hours per week available to work (no fewer than twenty-five). Applicants must also indicate date and place of birth, social security number, current address, and a reliable telephone number. If you are interested in interning with a particular section of USTR, indicate this in your cover letter. Such areas include agriculture, Asia and the Pacific, Canada and Mexico, congressional affairs, Europe and the Mediterranean, GATT affairs, General Counsel, Geneva, industry, Japan, China and Mongolia, Latin America, multilateral trade negotiations, policy coordination, private and public sectors, services and investment, and textiles.

The deadline for fall internship applications is 15 August, for spring internships 30 November, and for summer internships 15 March. Send information to:

Office of the United States Trade Representative
Attn: Public Affairs
600 17th Street, NW
Washington, DC 20506
(202) 395-3230

The **Central Intelligence Agency (CIA)*** coordinates the nation's intelligence activities by collecting, evaluating, and disseminating intelligence that directly affects our national security. The agency correlates the efforts of many federal intelligence organizations and provides the president and other policymakers with the information they need to formulate foreign policy.

The *Undergraduate Scholar Program* offers graduating high school students, particularly minorities and people with disabilities, who have a financial need for tuition assistance the opportunity to work with the CIA each college summer. Talented, highly motivated students with a strong academic record are encouraged to apply. Students who maintain a GPA of 2.75 or better receive tuition assistance (including tuition, fees, and books) and a salary throughout their college career. Students who complete the program are expected to continue employment with the agency after graduation for a period of one and one half times the length of their college career (six years if college is completed in four years.)

The *Minority Undergraduate Studies Program* provides promising undergraduate students, particularly minorities and people with disabilities, the opportunity to gain practical summer work experience to complement their academic studies. While earning competitive incomes, students are given the opportunity to work with a highly professional staff and participate in substantive work assignments corresponding with their academic training.

Student Trainees are mainly selected from academic institutions with established cooperative education programs. As part of the program, students work on an alternating semester or quarter basis and typically spend a minimum of three work periods of the job prior to graduation. Student trainees also receive competitive income during work periods.

The *Graduate Studies Program* is available for first and second year graduate students. It provides an opportunity for graduate students to work at the professional level, applying their college training and receiving competitive compensation while gaining significant work experience. To be eligible for this program, you must be committed to attend graduate school on a full-time basis following your internship. Most graduate fellows intern in the summer; however, fall and spring internships are also options.

Applicable majors include, but are not limited to, cartography, computer science, economics, engineering, foreign area studies, geography, graphic design/arts, international studies, management information systems, mathematics, non-romantic languages, photo sciences, and political science.

All positions are located in the Washington, D.C./Northern Virginia area. Most students receive round-trip transportation to Washington, D.C., and housing assistance is also provided. Students receive many of the same benefits as permanent employees, and their salaries are competitive with those paid in the private sector. Participating students are eligible to apply for the Agency's Tuition Assistance Program. Early application is needed to give adequate time for the lengthy six- to nine-month processing time. Students should send a current resume with cover letter to one of the following addresses:

> Coordinator for Student Programs
> Department S. 4N20J
> PO Box 1925
> Washington, DC 20013

> Personnel Representative
> PO Box 38428
> Denver, CO 80238
> (800) 562-7242

Domestic-Oriented Agencies

The **Federal Bureau of Investigation (FBI)*** is the federal government's principal agency responsible for investigating violations of more than 260 statues. The overall objective of the FBI is to investigate criminal activity and civil matters in which the federal government has an interest and to provide the executive branch with information relating to national security. FBI activities include investigations into organized crime, white-collar crime, public corruption, financial crime, fraud against the government, bribery, copyright matters, civil rights violations, bank robbery extortion, kidnapping, air piracy, terrorism, foreign counterintelligence, interstate criminal activity, fugitive and drug trafficking matters, and other violations of federal statutes. Today's FBI consists of over 9,500 special agents, assisted by over 13,000 specialty, technical, and clerical personnel.

The FBI sponsors an *Honors Internship Program* each summer for a select group of individuals. The purpose of the program is to expose a number of outstanding undergraduate and graduate students to the

FBI to promote their future interest in the bureau. At the same time, the program is also designed to enhance the FBI's visibility and recruitment efforts at a variety of colleges and universities throughout the United States.

Candidates for internships must be either undergraduates who have completed three years of college or graduate students. Applicants should have a 3.0 GPA on a 4.0 scale and meet other requirements for FBI employment, including U.S. citizenship. Individuals possessing strong academic credentials, outstanding character, a high degree of motivation, and the ability to represent the FBI upon return to their various campuses will be selected. The FBI seeks students with backgrounds in accounting, computer science, engineering, foreign languages, law, political science, and the physical sciences. Interns are paid at the GS 6 level although interns are responsible for travel expenses and housing.

If you are interested in this program, contact the applicant coordinator at the address below or a recruiter at the nearest FBI field office. The deadline for applications is 15 November each year.

Federal Bureau of Investigation
Personnel Resources
10th and Pennsylvania Avenue, NW
Room 6329
Washington, DC 20535
(202) 324-4991

The **Library of Congress** serves agencies of the federal government, other libraries, the scholarly community, and the general public. It offers a number of special employment programs for recent or soon-to-be graduates. The **Congressional Research Service** is responsible for providing Congress with research, analysis, and reference assistance, without partisan bias, in support of its legislative and representative functions.

The Library of Congress's *Graduate Recruit Program* offers a three-month appointment with possible permanent placement based upon performance, funding, and availability. Candidates should be enrolled in a master's or Ph.D. program in one of the following: biological/physical sciences, business administration, economics, international relations, law, library science, political science, public policy, or other appropriate fields.

The *Graduate Cooperative Education Program* offers three- to four-month initial appointments with the possibility of a thirteen-month indefinite appointment upon completion of a graduate degree. Candidates should be enrolled in an advanced degree program related to one of the following occupations: librarian social science analyst, economist, foreign affairs analyst, legislative attorney, administrative officer, and computer science analyst.

The *Foreign and Defense Policy Research Associate Program* hires groups of five temporary analysts for three-month appointments, year-round. Candidates must be nominated by the dean of a graduate program that provides extensive training in foreign and/or defense policy, or by a director of a foreign and/or defense policy research organization that employs significant numbers of graduate student-level research assistants.

The *Federal Research Division Foreign Area Associates Program* is designed to give students an opportunity to gain experience in fields related to foreign area studies and to use their foreign language skills. Candidates for this three-month appointment should major in foreign area studies, political science, modern foreign languages, foreign affairs/international relations, economics, history, military science/national security studies, or geography. For more information, contact:

Recruitment and Placement Office
Department E
Library of Congress
101 Independence Avenue, SE LM 107
Washington, DC 20540
(202) 707-5620/6295 (internship/job vacancy information)

The **National Security Agency** is the Department of Defense agency responsible for U.S. communications security. The agency has three areas: Signals Intelligence (SIGINT), which collects and analyzes foreign electromagnetic signals; Information Systems Security (INFOSEC), which protects U.S. telecommunications and computer systems against exploitation; and Operations Security (OPSEC), which trains U.S. government organizations to better secure their own operations. The NSA has a limited number of co-op and summer positions in mathematics, languages, computer science, and electrical or computer engineering. Co-op interns may be involved in building a special purpose computer radar system, programing or designing software systems, conducting research in communications, or transcribing, translating, and analyzing matter related to national security. Participants in the NSA Summer

Employment Program work the summer following their junior year in similar assignments.

Co-op interns must be enrolled in a university or college cooperative education program and have at least a 3.0 GPA on a 4.0 scale (math students should have a 3.5 GPA and have earned at least a 700 on the Math SAT). Interns and their immediate family must be U.S. citizens. Language co-op interns must be majoring in an Asian, Middle Eastern, or Slavic language.

NSA conducts its internships, or "work tours," on an alternating program: each work tour is alternated with a semester at school until a minimum of fifty-two weeks of work experience at the agency has been completed prior to graduation. Work tours are rotational, and the student changes areas within the agency for each tour in order to obtain the widest variety of experience. The first work tour is assigned according to agency need and the student's background, interest, and academic status. Tours thereafter increase in responsibility and difficulty, with the student having input in the tour selection. Students receive travel and tuition reimbursement. Salaries are determined by the percentage of credits completed toward a degree. For information, contact:

Cooperative Education Coordinator
National Security Agency
ATTN: M3222
Fort Meade, MD 20755-6000
(800) 962-9398
(410) 859-4590

Through the **Presidential Management Intern Program**, up to four hundred students who have completed their master's programs are invited each year to serve a two-year internship. Interns have a chance to find a career that matches their area of specialization and interest, since virtually every type of occupation exists within the federal government. In most agencies, positions range from generalist to specialist and include areas such as computer science, finance, health care/public health, international relations, natural resources, personnel, policy or management analysis, procurement, and program management, to name only a few. Although participation in the internship does not guarantee further employment, interns can move into regular civil service appointments without further competition.

The starting salary for *Presidential Management Interns* (PMIs) is $27,789 per year (GS-9) and includes eligibility for federal government benefits. After successful completion of the first year, PMI's are eligible for promotion to a salary level of $33,623 (GS-11). Upon completion of the two-year internships, PMI's are eligible for non-competitive conversion to career or career-conditional status and are eligible for promotion to GS-12 ($40,299). Salaries are 8 percent higher in New York City, San Francisco, and Los Angeles. (All salaries quoted are for 1993.)

Application materials are made available to graduate schools in early fall. Nominations should be made by the college or university official who has an appropriate knowledge of the nominee's abilities and achievements. In cases where an academic degree-granting program constitutes its own graduate school, nominations should come from the school dean. When an academic degree-granting program does not constitute its own school, nominations should come from the academic program director or chairperson. Nominations from individual professors, advisors, or placement counselors will not be accepted. Applications must be received by 1 December of each year.

For information on the PMI program, contact your graduate school dean, college placement office, or the nearest U.S. Office of Personnel Management (OPM) Regional Office. To obtain an application form, call the Career America Connection (912) 757-3000. In Alaska and Puerto Rico, call (912) 471-3755. Or write:

US Office of Personnel Management
Washington Area Service Center
1900 E Street, NW, Room 2458
Washington, DC 20415-0001

Nominees undergo a rigorous, competitive, two-tiered screening process. The first stage involves a comprehensive application review conducted by a panel of distinguished academic and government officials. The second step is a regional screening competition, which includes group and individual exercises, and a writing sample assignment. PMI finalists are notified of their selection at the end of March. In 1993, approximately 1,169 nominations were received from over 230 academic institutions.

United Nations

Although the United Nations seldom recruits paid staff for the summer months, ad hoc unpaid semester internships for currently enrolled graduate students who believe in the principles and activities of the United Nations can be arranged. In exceptional cases, senior undergraduate students may also act as interns. The purpose of the program is to promote among the participants a better understanding of major problems confronting the world and to give them insight into how the United Nations attempts to find solutions to these problems. The program also provides departments at headquarters with the assistance of outstanding young students specializing in relevant fields, such as international relations, international law, economics, political science, journalism, social affairs, population studies, translation and terminology, and public administration.

Candidates must be nominated by their sponsoring college or institution, who will complete part of the intern's application form. Applicants should also submit an essay, written in English or French, stating the purpose of the internship. Grade transcripts and a sample of research work in English or French should accompany the application. The UN Internship Program consists of three two-month periods through the year: mid-January to mid-March, mid-May to mid-July, and mid-September to mid-November.

Interns spend four days a week in that department or office of the Secretariat that has selected them for an internship, carrying out their assignment under the supervision of a staff member. In exceptional cases, individual internships may be extended one month.

For information and an application form, contact:

Internship Coordinator
Professional Staffing Services
Room S-2500E
United Nations
New York, NY 10017
(212) 963-1234/1224

The **United Nations Association of the USA** is a nonprofit, nonpartisan national organization designed to strengthen the UN system and enhance U.S. participation in the United Nations. Internships are available in the Economic Policy Council, Field Department, Model UN/Youth Department, Multilateral Studies, NY Chapter and Division, and Publications. Interns assist in research and writing of papers and books and respond to public inquiries. Unpaid internships are available to high school graduates, college sophomores, graduate students, and international applicants. Application deadline is 1 April for summer; 19 August for fall, 15 January for spring. For information, contact:

Intern Coordinator
United Nations Association of the USA
485 Fifth Avenue
New York, NY 10017-6104
(212) 697-3232

The **United Nations Department of Public Information (UNDPI)** offers *Graduate Student Intern Programs* in New York and Geneva on an annual basis. The New York program is held for a four to five-week period in June and July; it is conducted in English only. The program in Geneva is normally held for two and a half weeks in July or August; it is conducted in both English and French. These programs enable participants to obtain firsthand practical experience in the operations of the world's largest program of multilateral technical assistance in developing countries.

To qualify for an internship, students must satisfy UNDP's minimum educational and language requirements: they must be a student at the post-graduate level in development-related studies, be proficient in two of UNDP's main working languages (English, French, and Spanish), and have demonstrated a keen interest in the field of development.

Candidates should apply in writing through their college or university, using the application form that is generally available in the office of the dean of the relevant graduate schools at each participating institution. The closing date for the receipt of nominations from the sponsors is 28 February for the New York program and 25 April for the Geneva program. Applications for the New York program should be addressed to the first address below; applications for the Geneva program should be sent to the second address:

Coordinator of the DPI Graduate Student Intern Program
Department of Public Information
Room S-955
United Nations
New York, NY 10017

Information Service
United Nations Office at Geneva
Palais des Nations
CH-1211 Geneva 10
SWITZERLAND

The **United Nations Development Program (UNDP)*** is the fourth largest volunteer organization in the world. It sponsors five thousand development projects in 152 developing countries. In addition to its headquarters in New York, UNDP has an office in Washington, D.C., that accepts volunteer interns on a flexible year-round basis. Although internships are unpaid, a travel allowance is given to interns.

Interns should have an interest in development programs and may also find it helpful to know Spanish or French. For information, contact:

UN Development Program
Washington Office
1889 F Street, NW
Ground Floor
Washington, DC 20006
(202) 289-8674

The **United Nations Industrial Development Organization (UNIDO)*** was established in Vienna in 1967 to promote and accelerate the industrialization of developing countries by providing assistance to them at their request. Interns should have a background in administration, economics, industrial engineering, or management sciences. Language proficiency in English or French, as well as other UNIDO languages (Arabic, Chinese, Russian, and Spanish) is desirable. For information, contact:

New York Liaison Office
One UN Plaza DC1-1110
New York, NY 10017
(212) 963-1234

Ms. B. Sladek
Room G0666
Vienna International Centre
PO Box 300
1400 VIENNA

The **United Nations Institute for Training and Research (UNITAR)*** accepts a small number of visiting scholars and interns for work in research and training for periods varying between two months and one year. Applications should be sent through the appropriate Permanent Mission or directly from the sponsoring university or institute.

Executive Director of UNITAR
801 UN Plaza
New York, NY 10017

UNITAR
Palais des Nations
CH-1211 Geneva 10
SWITZERLAND

Assistance, Relief, and Development Organizations

Many organizations are supported almost completely by their volunteers, which means that the demand for volunteers is great and the competition somewhat less, although it still exists. Nonprofit organizations generally operate using salaried employees with some volunteers; whereas, volunteer organizations operate using volunteers with some salaried positions (generally administrative). Nonprofit organizations may occasionally offer paid internships. Unpaid volunteer internships are more frequent.

The following organizations and those listed under "Educational and Cultural Exchange Organizations" and "Research Institutions" are just a few of the various organizations that sponsor volunteer services in the area of assistance and relief, educational and cultural exchange, and research. The function, goal, and purpose of each organization may vary widely, which allows you to find your own niche. Some groups engage in assisting local firms to market projects overseas, coordinating foreign exchange programs, promoting mutual understanding, assisting nations and peoples in need, and providing information to travelers.

ACCION International works to combat unemployment and poverty by providing small business loans and technical training to small businesses in Latin America, the Caribbean, and the Southwestern United States. ACCION has three offices in the United States, but it does not hire for its overseas offices, which are employed by host country nationals. ACCION at times offers unpaid volunteerships, usually lasting six months to one year. Interns work seven to fifteen hours a week. The ability to speak Spanish is essential. Candidates should also have a knowledge of Spanish and Latin America, strong organizational skills, flexibility, and computer skills. According to the needs of the office, experience in other areas may be useful. Send cover letter and resume to:

Communications Specialist
130 Prospect Street
Cambridge, MA 02139
(617) 492-4930

Amnesty International USA is a worldwide human rights movement that works impartially for the release of prisoners of conscience, fair trials for political prisoners, and an end to torture and executions. Amnesty International USA's Washington Office presents Amnesty's concerns about human rights abuses to U.S. government officials, calling upon them to use their influence to press for human rights improvements in the United States and around the world.

Four world region internships are available: Africa, Asia, Europe and Middle East. Interns attend congressional hearings, compile materials from Amnesty International reports for briefing government officials, attend meetings with other human rights representatives, and answer requests for human rights information. Interns work with a variety of special projects, media/public relations, and legislation.

Most internships require a minimum commitment of thirty hours per week for ten weeks (shorter internships are possible in January and May). Interns should possess strong written and verbal communication skills, be familiar with Amnesty International and human rights issues, work well both as part of a team and independently, and be capable of taking on significant responsibility.

The deadline for summer internships is 1 April. Fall internships may be applied for at any time. Send (or fax) cover letter and resume, writing sample, and two letters of recommendation to the address below. Include dates you are available for an internship, the days per week you could work, as well as the specific internship in which you are interested.

Office Manager
Amnesty International USA
Washington Office
304 Pennsylvania Avenue, SE
Washington, DC 20003
(202) 544-0200
(202) 546-7142 FAX

A second Amnesty International office is located in Washington, D.C., whose responsibilities are to develop and support membership and to educate the public. For information, contact:

Mid-Atlantic Regional Office
1118 22d Street, NW
Washington, DC 20037
(202) 775-5161

Bread for the World is a nonpartisan Christian citizens' movement that works to end hunger. It does not distribute food, but rather acts as a lobbying force against world hunger. With an informed network of concerned Christians in every congressional district, Bread for the World gets the attention of the nation's leaders, helping to create policies that benefit hungry and poor people.

Paid and unpaid internships that last from three months to two years are available. Interns may work in a variety of areas: accounting, production of materials, including educational materials, and more. Some interns work with the media and church leaders across the broad denominational spectrum. Applicants should have a knowledge and interest in developing countries. Also useful is a background in nutrition, public relations, communications, administration, or accounting, as well as skills in writing, research, and public relations. The deadline for summer is 1 March, for fall is 1 June, for Winter/Spring is 1 October. For information, contact:

Bread for the World
1100 Wayne Avenue
Suite 1000
Silver Springs, MD 20910
(301) 608-2400

Cooperative for American Relief Everywhere (CARE)* is a nonprofit, nonsectarian independent relief and development organization. Its purpose is to help the developing world's poor in their efforts to achieve social and economic well-being. It offers technical assistance, training, food, and other material resources and management to local needs and priorities. Volunteer interns should have a background knowledge in such areas as agriculture, health care and nutrition, project management, and engineering. Previous work experience in a developing country and a knowledge of a second language are preferred. Volunteers, however, are not sent overseas; they work in the United States.

> CARE International Employment
> 151 Ellis Street
> Atlanta, GA 30303
> (404) 661-2552
>
> CARE Washington Liaison Office
> 2025 I Street, NW, Suite 1001
> Washington, DC 20006
> (202) 223-2277

The **Peace Corps** sends volunteers overseas on two-year assignments to help people in less-developed countries improve their standard of living. Because the Peace Corps does not generally require previous international experience, it is a readily accessible opportunity to gain valuable and necessary training; however, education and pertinent training are preferred. The Peace Corps also offers an enriching experience to fully trained specialists with a desire to volunteer their services.

Volunteers are needed in virtually every field from nutrition to conservation, from small business enterprises to construction. Although participants are not salaried employees, they receive a monthly living allowance, benefits, and travel expenses. In addition, they receive language and cultural training. RPCV (returned PC volunteers) also receive a "readjustment allowance" of about $5,000 and are eligible for various educational programs and government positions. Contact:

> Peace Corps Public Response Unit
> 9th Floor
> 1990 K Street, NW
> Washington, DC 20526
> (202) 606-3214
> (800) 424-8580

Visions in Action is an international nonprofit organization that coordinates volunteer internships in urban areas of developing countries. It is a nonsectarian, nonpolitical organization currently operating programs in Kenya, Uganda, Zimbabwe, South Africa, Burkina Faso, and India.

Interns may work in health care, business, journalism, to name only a few. Fluency in French or African languages is useful but not required (except in Burkina Faso); language training is provided. Visions in Action works primarily with small, local organizations, but it may also place interns with the United Nations, the local ministry of commerce and industry, and the largest newspaper in Kenya.

Interns receive a small stipend but take an active role in developing their own funds for their expenses using the Visions in Action fundraising information package. Internships last from six months to one year. For more information, contact:

Visions in Action
3637 Fulton Street, NW
Washington, DC 20007
(202) 625-7403

Educational and Cultural Exchange Organizations

AMIDEAST (America-Mideast Educational and Training Services, Inc.) is a nonprofit organization promoting cooperation and understanding between Americans and the people of the Middle East and North Africa through education, information, and development programs. Headquartered in Washington, D.C., AMIDEAST has a network of field offices located in Egypt, Jordan, Lebanon, Morocco, Syria, Tunisia, the West Bank/Gaza, and Yemen.

Unpaid internships generally provide administrative support to staff managing U.S. educational and training programs for foreign students from the Washington, D.C., office, staff producing publications and other materials for public in Washington, D.C., or staff advising Arab students about U.S. higher education in a field office overseas.

Most applicants are students in Arab/Middle East studies, international education, or international development. Arabic or French language proficiency, strong written and spoken English skills, and cross-cultural living, work, or study experiences are preferred. Modest stipends may be available for interns with special skills. Some interns are hired later as regular staff. For overseas internships, apply directly to field office directors. Send a cover letter explaining your interests and abilities with your resume and two references to:

Personnel Director
America-Mideast Educational and Training Services, Inc.
(AMIDEAST)
1100 17th Street, NW
Washington, DC 20036
(202) 785-0022

The **American Field Service (AFS)*** Intercultural Programs is the largest international high school exchange program in the world. Over sixty countries and eight thousand American and foreign students participate yearly. Unpaid internships are available in area studies, international program administration, research in intercultural learning, finance, marketing, public relations, publications, fundraising, personnel, and program support.

Interns should be sophomores, juniors, seniors, or graduate students with a minimum GPA of 2.5 on a 4.0 scale. Interns work two to three days a week. Students receive a stipend for lunch and transportation. Internships are offered spring (January-June), summer (June-August), and fall (September-January). For information, contact:

AFS Intercultural Programs
220 E 42d Street 3d Floor
New York, NY 10017
(212) 949-4242 ext. 538

Ashoka: Innovators for the Public is a nonprofit development organization that gives fellowships to individuals with creative ideas for social change in Asia, Latin America, and Africa. Interns write press releases, make travel plans, and prepare fund-raising proposals. Interns should have an interest in Third World development work and overseas experience with proficiency in a language (Spanish, French, Portuguese, Bahasa Indonesian, and Thai are preferred, although French, Nepali, and Bengali are also desirable). Interns must have proven research and writing skills as well as the ability to work independently.

The development and communications internships include the following: The *press/publications assistant* writes and edits press releases, and works to develop a communications and media strategy. The *fundraising assistant* researches foundation and corporate giving programs, takes on special projects, plans travel arrangements. The *in-kind fund raising coordinator* organizes the donation campaign, including training volunteers, developing contact list, and organization pickup and delivery of donations.

The *Ashoka Fellowship Resource Center Interns* provide resources to Ashoka Fellows, answer information requests, assist in research and writing of publications, provide administration support, and perform outreach and networking activities. A cover letter and a resume for these internships should be sent to the attention of the Director of the Fellowship Research Center at the address below. Development and communications internships described above should be to the address below.

Ashoka: Innovators for the Public
1700 North Moore Street, Suite 1920
Arlington, VA 22209
(703) 527-8300

The **China Institute in America** promotes American understanding of China through workshops, exchange programs, and films. Chinese language skills are not required for all positions but are helpful for some. Internships are available during the school year and summer depending on projects and initiatives developed. Interns work two to three full days a week rather than part days. Stipend and travel subsidy are available. Send a cover letter and a resume to:

Manager of Administration and Development
China Institute in America
125 East 65th Street
New York, NY 10021
(212) 744-8181

The **Council on International Educational Exchange (CIEE)** is a private, nonprofit, membership organization, incorporated in the United States, with international offices, affiliations, and representation. The council provides counseling and information services, conducts research and publishes studies, reports, and books; organizes conferences, seminars, and workshops; and plans projects to assist individuals, universities, and other organizations on matters of international education. It also offers many services to facilitate student and youth travel, study, and work abroad opportunities.

An educator exchange program is also available, as are international internships and short-term summer programs for volunteers. For teachers, a year of teaching experience and a current teaching certificate, plus language fluency, are required (private schools may not require certification). Applicants should have a minimum of a bachelor's degree and language ability, as well as some international experience. Internships are available to college students, sophomore or above. For information, contact:

Council on International Educational Exchange
205 East 42d Street
New York, NY 10017
(212) 661-1414

The **Middle East Institute** is a nonprofit organization dedicated to improving public knowledge and understanding of the region from Morocco through Central Asia to Pakistan. The institute seeks to fulfill its mission by offering lectures and conferences; providing language instruction in Arabic, Hebrew, Persian, and Turkish; publishing the *Middle East Journal*; and operating the George Camp Keiser Library. The institute does not take positions on issues of public policy, nor does it seek to influence legislation. Rather, the institute strives to offer a forum for the expression, study, and discussion of a variety of viewpoints.

Internships are available with the Educational and Cultural Programs Department, the Political and Economic Programs Department, as well as with the *Middle East Journal*. Interns may plan and administer lectures, conferences, language courses, and publications. *Journal* interns proofread book reviews, draft annotations of books for publications, and take part in the process of producing a scholarly journal.

Unpaid internships are available throughout the year, corresponding with the autumn spring, and summer academic semesters. Some internships are full time, others part time to complement school work or other employment. Although interns are not paid, they are reimbursed for local commuting costs and are eligible to take one language course tuition-free through the institute. Interns may also attend congressional briefings.

European and Middle Eastern languages are helpful in some positions but are not required for all. Candidates should have some formal course work in the area they apply to work in. Good English language skills are required; although, the institute is not a research-oriented organization. Organizational and word processing skills are helpful.

Send letter, resume, writing sample, college transcript, and a letter of recommendation to:

Internship Coordinator
Middle East Institute
1761 N Street, NW
Washington, DC 20036-2882
(202) 785-0191

Youth for Understanding (YFU)* is an international nonprofit educational exchange organization that coordinates semester-long exchange programs between high school students and host families. With seven thousand students and host families, YFU operates in about forty countries, with the assistance of over three thousand volunteers. YFU provides cross-cultural orientation, counseling, and language assistance for program participants and runs the world's leading international youth sports exchange program, Sport for Understanding (SFU). Teams, led by trained volunteer coaches, travel abroad each year, representing nearly two dozen different sports. Foreign teams, hosted by SFU, also travel to the United States.

Unpaid internships are available in a variety of positions. The *Public Relations Intern* writes news releases and articles for internal and external newsletters. The *International Publications and Research Assistant* edits the YFU international newsletter and produces the international student program. The *Corporate Development Intern* writes articles for the corporate newsletter. The *School Relations Intern* reviews aspects of school relations projects/programs, summarizes educational material and events, and acts as liaison for educators interested in YFU information. The *Community College Program Intern* in the School Relations Office assists in the design of participant program evaluations and in the maintenance of program correspondence and administrative files. For all of these positions, strong writing and computer skills are required. A background in international affairs is preferred.

The *YFU/Kellogg Mexico–U.S. Project Intern* (School Relations Office) conducts preliminary review of school applications for the student exchange and teacher training in Mexico and assists in on-going communications with participating schools. Cross-cultural experience in Latin America and a strong interest in education and/or U.S.–Mexican relations is preferred.

The *Financial Assistant to the Controller* assists in payroll and travel account processing, accounts payable and receivable, and special projects. Interns need computer experience and a background in accounting theory, auditing, and finance analysis.

SFU offers the following internships: *Management Assistant*, who assists in developing national and international contacts interested in Youth Sport Exchanges and assists with a coaches' workshop; and *Marketing and Promotional Assistant*, who assists in developing sports contacts for the SFU program nationwide and in the implementation of selected marketing and recruitment strategies for specific sports and countries. Experience in sports, marketing, or international relations is preferred. Staff positions are available for individuals with degrees in international affairs or related fields.

Interns generally work a flexible twelve to twenty-hour work week. College credit can be obtained. Local transportation costs are reimbursed. For more information, contact:

Coordinator, Intern Program
Youth for Understanding
3501 Newark Street, NW
Washington, DC 22016-20016
(202) 966-6808

Research Institutions

American Enterprise Institute for Public Policy Research (AEI)* is a private, nonpartisan research institution dedicated to preserving and improving the institutions of a free society, which is defined as an open and competitive private enterprise, limited and public-spirited government, strong and well-managed defense and foreign policies, and vital cultural and political values. AEI is home to some of America's most renowned economists, legal scholars, political scientists, and foreign policy experts.

Research Assistants in the Foreign Policy department provide research support to the scholars on staff at AEI. Students who intern also assist Foreign Policy experts. Paid summer internships as research assistants are available. Contact the Washington Seminar Office (see Appendix) or send a cover letter and a resume to:

American Enterprise Institute
Personnel Office
1150 17th Street, NW
Washington, DC 20036
(202) 862-5800

The **Hudson Institute** is a nonprofit policy research "think tank" that conducts research studies on a wide range of international economic, political, and security issues, and is particularly known for its work in Soviet and East European studies, Asian studies, Western European political and military affairs, and Latin American studies.

Applicants for internships, mainly unpaid, should have solid regional expertise, including knowledge of the region's principal language(s) or a very strong background in a functional field, such as economics or national security studies. For information, contact:

Hudson Institute
Herman Kahn Center
PO Box 26-919
Indianapolis, IN 46226
(317) 545-1000

The **Institute for International Economics (IIE)** studies international economic policy. Research assistantships are available to college graduates with language and computer skills, good statistical analysis skills, and an international background. Send a cover letter and a resume to:

Assistant to the Director
Institute for International Economics
11 Dupont Circle, NW, Suite 620
Washington, DC 20036
(202) 328-0583

The **Overseas Development Council (ODC)** is a "think tank" that seeks to promote American understanding of problems in developing countries. Research efforts are discussed in conferences and publications. Candidates should have a background in economics or international relations along with computer and research skills. Send a cover letter and a resume to:

Overseas Development Council
1875 Connecticut Avenue, Suite 1012
Washington, DC 20009
(202) 234-8701

Resources for Potential Internships

If books are not available at a local library or university placement office, they can be ordered from the publisher. A longer resource list is given at the end of the guide. Where possible, phone numbers are included.

Associations

National Society for Internships and Experiential Education (NSIEE), 3509 Haworth Drive, Suite 207, Raleigh, NC 27609. (919) 787-3263.

Directories

Directory of International Careers. 1991. Francis M. Jeffries. Jeffries & Associates, 17200 Hughes Road, Poolesville, MD 20837. (301) 972-8034.

Directory of International Internships: A World of Opportunities. 1990. 2d ed. Comps. and eds. Thomas D. Luten, Charles A. Gliozzo, and Timothy J. Aldinger. Available from Michigan State University, Career Development and Placement Service, 113 Student Services Building, East Lansing, MI 48824. Attn: International Placement. (517) 355-9510 ext. 164. ($20 postpaid.)

Directory of Internships, Work Experience Programs, and On-the-Job Training Opportunities. 1990. 2d ed. Ready Reference Press, Box 5169, Santa Monica, CA 90405.

International Directory of Voluntary Work. 1991. David Woodworth. Peterson's Guides. (800) EDU-DATA.

The National Directory of Corporate Training Programs. 1988. Ray Bard and Susan K. Elliott. Bantam Doubleday Dell Publishing Group, 1540 Broadway, New York, NY 10036. (800) 223-6834.

National Directory of Internships. 1992. 8th ed. Eds. Barbara E. Baker and Bridget B. Millsaps. NSIEE, 3509 Haworth Drive, Suite 207, Raleigh, NC 27609. (919) 787-3263.

Yearbook of International Organizations 1990-91. 1990. 3 vols. Reed Reference Publishing, K. G. Saur, 121 Chanlon Road, New Providence, NJ 07974. (800) 521-8110.

Publications

The Experienced Hand: A Student Manual for Making the Most of an Internship. 1987. Timothy K. Stanton and Kamil Ali. NSIEE, 3509 Haworth Drive, Suite 207, Raleigh, NC 27609. (919) 787-3263.

Internships in Foreign & Defense Policy: A Complete Guide for Women (& Men). 1990. Prepared by Women in International Security (WIIS), the Center for International Security Studies. Published by Seven Locks Press, Cabin John, Maryland, Washington, DC. (301) 320-2130.

Internships 1992: On-the-Job Training Opportunities for Students & Adults. 1992. 12th ed. Peterson's Guides, PO Box 2123, Princeton, NJ 08543-2123. (800) 338-3282.

1992 Washington D.C. Internship Directory: Everything You Need to Know to Obtain an Internship in the Nation's Capital. 1991. Ed. Diane Chingren Boyd. A project of the Congressional Youth Leadership Council, 1511 K Street NW, Suite 842, Washington, DC 20005. (202) 638-0008.

Volunteer! The Comprehensive Guide to Voluntary Service in the U.S. and Abroad. 1990-91 ed. Published by the Commission on Voluntary Service and Action and CIEE. Available from CIEE. 205 East 42d Street, New York, NY 10017. (212) 661-1414.

Volunteer Vacations. 1991. 3d ed. Rev. & expanded by Bill McMillon. Chicago Review, 814 North, Franklin Street, Chicago, IL 60610. (312) 337-0747.

SECTION 7
WHERE DO YOU GO TO FIND A JOB?

Today's competitive job market means that you've got to work harder then ever to get a job. Companies are downsizing and more people are looking for work.

It is not likely that you will find the "perfect" job right out of college; rather, you will find a job that offers many things you like—variety, a chance to learn, a good location. The important thing is not finding the one perfect job but having the opportunity to learn and gain experience.

Statistics show that most people change jobs seven to ten times in their lives, which means that the job search may often be harder than the job itself. However, you'll find it much easier if you network through friends, teachers, college counselors, family and relatives, and recruiters. Investigate your college placement, work study, and cooperative education offices. Visit your local job service and employment agencies in your area. Check out trade journals, bulletin boards, and job and career fairs.

Four Stages of the Job Hunter

Stage One: Confidence

You are finishing college and you're ready for a "real" job and a "real" salary. You took a resume class or went to a professional resume writer, so you feel set. You've made some contacts, you've talked to friends. You've even looked through several trade journals and newsletters for your field and sent off your applications after carefully constructing a cover letter. You feel in control of your fate and hopeful for the future.

While the techniques described above are good, they cannot alone guarantee your success. The job seeker at Stage One approaches the job market as a "buyer," "I'm looking for a job and I think I qualify. I'd like to fill out an application or send you my resume." At this stage, most job seekers haven't yet learned that it is the companies who are the buyers, which leads job seekers into Stage Two.

Stage Two: Frustration

The first month of job seeking, maybe even the second, wasn't too bad. But as you move into the third, fourth, and fifth months, you begin to feel discouraged. You look at your resume and wonder what is wrong. You have fewer interviews and you go into them feeling more anxious than you did at first.

Although you may have had a few job offers, they were below your salary expectations. Or perhaps after the interview, the job seemed less inviting. After so many interviews that don't pan out, or so many letters that don't lead to interviews, you start to wonder if you will ever find a job. You may even despair that you chose the "wrong" college major.

Stage Three: Doubt

A few months earlier, anything seemed possible. Now you wonder if you should just take whatever comes up next, just to get this whole thing over with.

Some believe that at this point, yes, you should take a job, preferably part time, which will allow you the time to keep looking and interviewing and at the same time pay the bills and give you a sense of accomplishment. However, some feel it unwise to commit themselves to a job they know is temporary or that will tie up their time.

No one likes to be rejected, and the job search is a line of No, No, No, No... followed at last by a single Yes. And until that yes comes, many job seekers can become overwhelmed by emotions of fear and rejection and lose their objectivity.

Stage Four: Relief

For many people, getting a job is pure perseverance. You may apply for a job six or seven times and not get hired until the eighth attempt. Some people receive a letter of rejection and instead of falling into depression, they call to ask their interviewer where they fell short. By continuing to express their willingness to start anywhere and work their way up, they received similar, though less well paying jobs that offered the potential to move up. Remember, all it takes is just one Yes.

Do It Right From the Beginning

Because of the extreme competitiveness of today's job market, job seekers need to become aware, starting at Stage One, that they are not shopping around for a job as buyers but are looking to sell their skills. And so as sellers, they want to market themselves with an eye to what the buyer—the employer—is looking for.

- Know your strengths and weakness. Know what you have to offer that will appeal to the employer. Know how to downplay your weakness.

- Position yourself correctly in the marketplace. Be where the jobs are.

- Develop the most visually appealing and effective marketing tools—including resume, cover letter, even your own appearance.

- Target the employers and decision makers for the companies you want.

- Distribute your materials for maximum exposure in minimum time.

- Establish your value and selling price. Be realistic. Don't sell yourself short but don't overprice yourself. (Salt Lake Tribune, Sunday, 24 Jan. 1993)

NOTE: If you haven't yet, now is the time to go back through the exercises in section one. By doing so, you will become better acquainted with your marketable skills and your overall employment objectives.

Section 8
Private Sector Opportunities

Getting Started in an International Job

Literally, thousands of companies have operations, contacts, branches, or clients in areas outside the United States. However, very few firms give entry-level employees immediate international responsibilities. Such assignments are generally given to experienced domestic employees or nationals, after a period of solid performance. Students desiring international work may eventually get it, but probably only after several years of domestic experience.

Dozens, if not hundreds, of corporations seek international affairs graduates who possess knowledge essential to that firm. Some businesses, for example, seek graduates with a knowledge of foreign, legal, and administrative systems or comparative economic systems. However, the student of international affairs should be aware that a firm grasp of marketing, finance, or accounting may be essential to obtain a job with a corporation. Internships or work experience are also valuable assets for the job seeker.

Rather than sending hundreds of resumes to international firms, your best bet may simply be to find a domestic company—one that has international branches, clients, etc., if possible but not necessarily—and begin working. Learn your field well, and gain a reputation for being a good worker. Continue to learn—another language, computer skills, etc.—and keep up on what is happening in the world by reading good journals and newspapers.

Other routes to finding international employment:

- Use a "shot gun" approach sending out resumes to every company you can think of.
- Go to an employment agency.
- Begin with a small, or domestic company and work up.

Whatever your choice, keep your resume updated, do your best work wherever you are, and keep your eyes open for those "windows of opportunity" that may open at any time.

If you can afford it, find an international unpaid volunteer internship that will allow you to use your area of expertise. Or, if you must work, another option is to volunteer locally one night a week. Still, another option is to start in a nonprofit organization, where you may have less competition since salaries are lower.

Resources for Private Sector Employment

Because hiring practices, career opportunities, and specific needs are not always consistent over time in the private sector, individual companies or organizations are not listed. A few general rules: try to gain as much internship experience as possible, read the trade journals, and learn as much as you can about the companies that you would like to work with. (Ask for an annual report from the company.)

The career guides and directories listed below offer information on different companies as well as on the entire job search process. Since companies and personnel change, and even job requirements may change frequently, contact each firm to inquire about its particular requirements.

Directories

Directory of American Firms Operating in Foreign Countries. 1991. 3 vols. Available at the library or through the World Trade Academy Press, 50 East 42d Street, Suite 509, New York, NY 10017. (212) 697-4999. Lists more than 3,200 U.S. companies operating in more than 120 countries.

Yearbook of International Organizations 1988-89. Union of International Associations. Brussells, Belgium.

Publications

Almanac of International Jobs and Careers. 1991. Ronald L. and Caryl L. Krannich. Impact Publications. (703) 361-7300.

Careers in International Affairs. 1991. Eds. Maria Pinto Carland and Daniel H. Spatz, Jr. Georgetown University, Institute for Study of Diplomacy School for Foreign Services, Washington, DC 20057-1052 (202) 687-8971.

The Complete Guide to International Jobs and Careers: Your Passport to a World of Exciting and Exotic Employment. 1992. Ronald L. and Caryl R. Krannich. Impact Publications. (703) 361-7300.

Exploring Careers Using Foreign Language. 1990. Rev. ed. E. W. Edwards. Ed. Ruth Rosen. Rosen Group, 29 East 21st Street, New York, NY 10010. (800) 237-9932.

Guide to Careers in World Affairs. 1993. Foreign Policy Association Editors, 729 7th Avenue, New York 10016. (800) 477-5836.

How to Be an Importer and Pay for Your World Travel. Rev. ed. no date. Mary Green and Stanley Gillmar, Ten Speed Press, Box 7123, Berkeley, CA 94707. (800) 841-2665.

International Jobs—Where They Are, How to Get Them: A Handbook for Over 500 Career Opportunities. 1989. (3d ed., rev.) Eric Kocher, Addison-Wesley Publishing. Reading, MA.

International Internships and Volunteer Programs. 1992. Will Cantrell & Francine Modderno. Worldwise Books. (703) 620-1972.

Looking for Employment in Foreign Countries. 1992. 9th ed. World Trade Academy Press. (212) 697-4999.

Making It Abroad —The International Job Hunting Guide. 1988. Howard Schuman, John Wiley & Sons, 605 Third Avenue, New York, NY 10158-0012. (800) 225-5945.

The Overseas List: Opportunities for Living and Working in Developing Countries. 1985. David M. Beckman, Timothy J. Mitchell, and Linda L. Powers. Minneapolis: Augsburg Fortress. 57 East Main Street, Columbus, OH 43215-5183. (800) 848-2738.

Section 9
Federal Government

The federal government is the nation's largest employer. In 1987 it employed three million workers (not including 2.1 million members of armed forces); most jobs (88 percent) are located outside of Washington, D.C. Federal jobs are very popular, so competition is intense, particularly in the Foreign Service.

Over 70 percent of all positions are offered through the Office of Personnel Management (OPM). Resumes should be sent to the OPM to receive a ranking, which is often necessary to apply for a position. However, a candidate must not rely solely on the OPM for hiring but should also directly contact the individual agencies. The OPM has fifty-four regional offices nationwide. Refer to the blue pages of your phone directory under U.S. Government for the appropriate address, or write to the OPM. (See the address listed below.)

The U.S. Office of Personnel Management offers a variety of services through the Federal Job Information Center to assist job seekers. This includes access to information specialists from 8:00 A.M.–4:00 P.M. and forms request capability at all times. Call the nearest OPM Area Office or Federal Job Information Center found in your telephone director under "U.S. Government," or call:

For recorded job information 7 days a week, 24 hours a day
(202) 606-2700

For people with disabilities
(202) 606-2528

For Telephone Device for the Deaf (TDD)
(202) 606-0591

For Career America College Hotline
(900) 990-9200 (cost is 40 cents per minute)

To learn about vacancies or recruitment programs, check bulletin boards in placement offices (agencies are required to post their openings) or at school and college guidance or placement offices. Look in the phone book under "U.S. Government," or check state employment offices. Occasionally newspapers or periodicals, friends employed by government, other commercially developed sources that list vacancies, such as those listed below, will also be helpful:

Federal Jobs Digest
325 Pennsylvania Avenue SE
Washington, DC 20003

Federal Employment Bulletin
 PO Box 11715
Washington, DC 20008

Federal Times
475 School Street SW
Washington, DC 20024

Federal Career Insights
PO Box 2059
Vienna, VA 22180

Applying for federal employment is a long and complex task, as
most jobs require an examination as well as a series of interviews. (The
OPM can explain what is necessary for each position.) For this reason,
begin the process at least a year before you want to start working. To
prepare for required examinations, talk to people who have taken them
and review official study guides.

Passing the test will place your name on a register. Names are taken
from this list when there are openings. If your name is chosen from a
register, you will interview with the agency hiring officials.

For application forms, write:

Office of Personnel Management
1900 E Street, NW
Washington, DC 20415-0001

*NOTE: After you complete the necessary applications, remember to
make copies for your own use.*

Many career opportunities exist in the U.S. government for qualified people with an international background. Some federal agencies
are foreign-oriented, while others are domestic-oriented but have foreign opportunities in their international divisions.

Because the hiring practices of most domestic agencies vary with
position, circumstances, or policy, it is difficult to detail application
procedures for each agency. For this reason, this section lists general
opportunities and qualifications, along with relevant addresses and

phone numbers where possible. Interested applicants should contact the agency for exact information relative to the division or position being applied for.

Note: As indicated earlier, addresses and phone numbers are subject to change. An asterisk (*) next to an agency means that this entry is cross referenced with a similar entry in the section on internships.

Foreign-Oriented Agencies

The **Foreign Service, Department of State**,* has four areas of specialization, or "cones," in the Foreign Service. The *Administrative* cone is concerned with management. Administration officers perform work in six different categories: budget, general services, personnel, security, communications, and information systems.

Accordingly, the work of an administration officer might include coordinating an overseas trip for the president, vice president, or secretary of state; making various arrangements for a congressional delegation; developing computer programs and communications systems; preparing a budget submission for Congress; negotiating with foreign customs officials; or preparing an emergency evacuation plan.

Administrative officers should be familiar with modern management tools including accounting, finance, data processing systems analysis, and operations research. An MBA or MPA degree is recommended.

The *Consular* cone provides services to Americans and foreigners abroad. Helping Americans involved in serious accidents abroad and handling passports and visas are among the functions performed by the consular officers. At the junior level, Foreign Service Officers (FSOs) abroad often gain management experience by supervising foreign national employees. At more senior levels, especially in big consular sections, consular officers have broad management responsibilities. In policy terms, consular officers are concerned with the movements of people. In service terms, the daily work focuses on visas for foreigners and assistance to fellow Americans overseas. Prospective consular officers should be service oriented and enjoy doing "casework."

The *Economic/Commercial* cone is concerned with protecting and advancing U.S. economic and commercial interests as well as U.S. trade and investment. In Washington, D.C., economic officers are concerned with issues involving trade, investment and monetary matters, and energy. In areas of economic development, aviation, transportation, food, and maritime matters, officers deal with other U.S. government agencies concerned with national and international economic policies, and with foreign embassies. Abroad, economic officers analyze and report on key economic trends and events that affect U.S. interests. They also brief visiting U.S. officials and escort them when necessary.

The *Political* cone is associated with traditional diplomatic work. Political officers analyze and report on political matters that affect U.S. interests. They convey U.S. government views on political issues to foreign officials, negotiate agreements, and maintain close contact with political and labor leaders, third-country diplomats, and others of influence. In Washington, D.C., political officers often work in offices specializing in the affairs of particular countries or regions. They analyze reports from overseas staff, prepare guidance for U.S. embassies, and brief senior Department of State officials. They work closely with other U.S. government agencies and with foreign embassies in Washington.

Every year, over fourteen thousand applicants take the Foreign Service Exam. About two thousand pass, and about one hundred to two hundred are granted positions. Because many fail to pass the first time, the exam may be taken repeatedly; most applicants improve with each try. In fact, many FSOs failed the examination on their first try.

If you are interested in the Foreign Service, applications must be received by mid-October. A required Foreign Service written exam is generally given in December each year. A booklet describing this exam and the work of the Foreign Service is usually available at university placement centers, or it can be obtained by writing to the address below.

The test is very broad in nature and no specific course of study can be used to prepare for it. The exam tests your general knowledge in such areas as art, history, economics, political science, western civilization, business management, and international affairs. Candidates should also have a good background in English and a basic understanding of economics. Those who pass the written examination are then eligible for a day-long oral assessment that consists of an oral examination, written exercises, a group exercise, and a written practical application exercise. The oral assessment is designed to evaluate your awareness of current political, economic, and cultural issues; oral communication skills; administrative/problem solving skills; leadership skills; and personal characteristics such as interpersonal skills, cultural awareness and sensitivity, stability, and resourcefulness. Assessments are given in Washington, D.C., and in a number of other major cities in the United States. Travel is at the candidate's expense.

A final review weighs a candidate's qualifications against those of other candidates. While knowledge of a foreign language is not required for appointment, all new officers must demonstrate professional competency in at least one foreign language before the end of their initial probationary period. Also, successful candidates with a knowledge of a foreign language, particularly an exotic or difficult language, receive higher entry-level salaries. Those hired without knowing a foreign language will be required to learn one. Members of the Foreign Service can expect to spend about half of their career time abroad.

The names of successful candidates are placed for eighteen months on a rank-order register from which the Foreign Service hires according to need. Being on the register does not guarantee a job offer. If one does not receive a position within this eligibility period, the applicant must restart the process.

Civil service employees also work for the Department of State and are regularly involved with international issues. They do not enter through the Foreign Service Exam but through the normal civil service channels. For more information, contact the Office of Personnel Management.

For test registration information, send a postcard to:

Foreign Service Examination
PO Box 12226
Arlington, VA 22219
(703) 875-7247

For applications and information, send a letter describing your particular areas of interest to:

US Department of State
Recruitment Division
Box 9317, Rosslyn Station
Arlington, VA 22219
(703) 875-7490/7198

Foreign Service Job Opportunities Hotline
(703) 875-7490

Civil Service Job Opportunities Hotline
(202) 647-7284

The **U.S. Agency for International Development (AID)*** is responsible
for the entire U.S. economic aid program to developing countries. Its
purpose is to help people in the developing world acquire the knowledge and resources to build the economic, political, and social institutions needed to maintain national development. This assistance covers
many diverse sectors including agriculture, food and nutrition, family
planning and health, education and human resources, energy, environment, natural resources, and private enterprise.

AID usually requires a minimum of two years related experience as
well as experience in a developing country. A graduate degree is
desirable. A foreign language is required for many positions, French
and Spanish being the most preferred. AID usually recruits for the
following positions:

The *program economist* conducts analyses of both the macroeconomic
conditions of host countries and the microeconomic feasibility of individual programs. The *private enterprise officer* designs and manages the
overall private sector strategy, developing financial systems and ex-
panding local, indigenous private sector activities. The *program officer*
advises the mission director and technical staff on AID program policy,
planning, and evaluation. The program development officer advises
and assists in the planning, analysis, negotiation, and implementation
of AID projects. A bachelor's degree in international relations, area
studies, development studies, public administration, political science,
economics, finance, or business is required. A graduate degree is
desirable.

The *financial management officer* maintains a comprehensive accounting system and provides financial and statistical data. The *administrative management officer* oversees a range of management and administrative support functions including personnel, contracting procurement, property management, and general services. A bachelor's in
accounting, business, public administration, or international management is required.

The *education/human resources development officer* analyzes, advises,
and assists with the development of host country education systems. A
background in one of the following fields is desirable: education,
psychology, sociology, anthropology, or communications, with specialized experience in educational research/evaluation, educational
administration, or curriculum development.

The *agriculture/rural development/natural resources officer* advises
senior AID and host government officials on agriculture, rural develop-

ment, or natural resources. A graduate degree in an agricultural specialty, rural development, or anthropology is required. Specialized experience in planning, design, implementation, and management of agriculture, rural development, or natural programs is desirable.

The *health/population/nutrition officer* assists host country leaders in designing and managing health delivery systems, population/family planning projects, and nutrition/feeding programs. A graduate degree in nursing or public health, an M.S. (with an emphasis in public health or nutrition), or nursing with experience in health care financing is desirable.

The *housing/urban development officer* assists in planning, designing, implementing, and monitoring AID's shelter programs in developing countries. A bachelor's degree in urban planning, economics, or finance is required.

For information on the above positions, contact:

Agency for International Development (AID)
Recruitment Division
2401 E Street, NW
Room 1026 SA-1
Washington, DC 20523-0116
(202) 663-2368

The **Central Intelligence Agency (CIA)*** has four directorates: Intelligence, Operations, Science and Technology, and Administration. Many believe the Operations directorate, responsible for clandestine activities and intelligence gathering, has the largest budget. However, the Intelligence directorate, which houses all analysts, carries over 90 percent of the budget. While analysts have advanced degrees, the Operations directorate will accept individuals with a bachelor's degree.

A bachelor's or advanced degree in political science, international relations, area studies, or the social sciences is required. Strong written and oral communications skills are essential. Foreign language ability or aptitude is desirable but not essential. Operations officers usually work under the diplomatic cover of another position at a U.S. embassy or consulate; some work in Washington, D.C.

The ability to speak a foreign language and experience living and traveling abroad are helpful to CIA applicants. While some opportunities to travel arise, most work is done in the Washington, D.C., area.

Those interested in applying to the CIA should contact their college placement center for an interview with a CIA personnel representative or send a resume directly to the CIA. Applicants passing the initial screening take an all-day exam; if successful, a series of tests is required in Washington, D.C. A security background investigation is also done. The process is a lengthy one, so apply well in advance of when you will be available to begin work. For information, write:

> Director of Personnel
> CIA
> Washington, DC 20505
> (703) 351-2141

The **Foreign Broadcast Information Service (FBIS)** is the office of the CIA that monitors foreign public media—radios, press agencies, television, newspapers, journals, and books—and disseminates the collected information to U.S. government agencies. It also provides analysis of foreign media and translations for various government agencies. Although FBIS is part of the CIA, most of its work is unclassified. Five types of career opportunities are available in FBIS.

Information officers (editors) organize and edit a news report issued five days a week; staff a twenty-four-hour overseas wire service; and manage field bureaus in some fifteen countries, monitoring radio and television news broadcasts around the world. Majors in English, history, international relations, area studies, and journalism are desirable, as is experience in news writing and editing or in teaching, supervisory, and leadership positions. Knowledge of a foreign language is not necessary because most work consists of editing the translations of foreign translators.

Information officers spend about half their career in foreign posts, so applicants must be willing to serve at any location at home or abroad. Work is often demanding because of the twenty-four-hour operation requirements.

Language officers scan foreign language publications for critical information needed by the foreign affairs community. This work consists primarily of selecting articles from the foreign press for translation by Joint Publications Research Service (JPRS) translators. A language officer edits translations, assigns tasks to other translators, and on occasion, translates urgently needed documents. There are also opportunities for transfer to other analytical offices of the CIA to provide language support. Applicants must have good English skills plus strong reading ability in one or more foreign languages. A degree in social or political science, area studies, or international relations is desirable.

Analysts interpret news developments and policy trends in the country in which they serve. They write weekly and special in-depth articles and analytical studies for U.S. policy makers. Applicants should have a graduate degree or equivalent experience in international relations or area studies or in the history of key countries. The ability to read newspaper and journal materials in the language or languages of these countries is desirable. Analysts are expected to produce cogently written articles or studies, often against short deadlines, as well as to conduct long-range research. Work is primarily in the Washington, D.C., area.

Engineers plan, design, install, and maintain foreign and domestic electronic receiving systems, satellites, terminals, and other communications systems. Electronics, electrical engineering, computer science, or similar scientific background is needed. Engineers work in Washington, D.C., and virtually every part of the world. Overseas assignments can be for a two-year tour or less for special projects.

Freelance Translators work through the JPRS at home as independent contractors and are paid by commission. Translators are needed to translate from some sixty foreign languages into English. U.S. citizenship is not required, but those hired must pass a security background investigation. One qualifies as a translator by passing a written test consisting of sample translations. JPRS is especially interested in translators who have mastered scientific or technical vocabularies. Pay is commensurate with the translator's educational background, experience, and level of accomplishment. Although there is currently an increasing demand for translators, the JPRS does not guarantee a continuous flow of work. For more information, write:

Foreign Broadcast Information Service
Box 2604
Washington, DC 20013

The **Department of Commerce** supervises the **Foreign Commercial Service (FCS)**, which is the government's international trade agency with a global field organization and delivery system, giving American business direct access to more than 95 percent of the world market for U.S. exports of goods and services. It also provides commercial attachés to American diplomatic missions.

Foreign Service Officers (FSOs) identify overseas business connections for American exporters and investors, conduct market research for American products, and organize trade promotion events. These FSOs combine the skills of an analyst, the resilience of a broker, and the imagination of an entrepreneur in building trade across cultural differences. For information and application forms, contact:

Recruitment Division
US Department of State
Box 9317, Rosslyn Station
Arlington, VA 22219
(703) 875-7490/7198
(800) JOB-OVERSEAS

The **U.S. Information Agency (USIA)*** promotes mutual understanding by providing information to citizens of foreign countries about American events and culture. Since most of the agency's work centers on public affairs, a background in communications media, such as journalism or cultural studies, is needed. A background in area studies, languages, foreign policy, international relations, and administration is also helpful.

USIA officers may serve as *information officers* or *cultural affairs officers*. An information officer is responsible for activities relating to the mass media and normally serves as an embassy press spokesman, responsible for much of the embassy's public relations work. The *information officer* may also analyze press coverage of an American official's visit or advise U.S. officials on a country's political climate. A *cultural affairs officer* administers educational and cultural exchange programs, arranges lectures and seminars with American speakers, manages American libraries, organizes exhibits, assists local publishers with reprints and translations of American books, and works closely with bilateral educational exchange organizations.

The **Voice of America (VOA)*** is also a responsibility of USIA. This radio network broadcasts news and information in forty-two languages to most countries of the world. Individuals wishing to work for VOA must have a degree in broadcast journalism. To apply for one of the positions listed in the recording, complete an SF-171 (application for federal government) and give the exact title of the position and the vacancy announcement number at the top (lines #1 and #2). If you wish to apply for several positions, you must submit a separate SF-171 for each position (clear photocopies are acceptable, but signatures must be original). Send your application to:

US Information Agency
Room 518
301 4th Street, SW
Washington, DC 20547
(202) 619-4539

Voice of America
Room 1543 Cohen Building
330 Independence Avenue, SW
Washington, DC 20547
(202) 619-0909

The **U.S. International Trade Commission** investigates matters of international trade and tariffs and provides technical assistance to the president, Congress, other government agencies, and the public on international trade issues. The commission employs attorneys, international economists, investigators, commodity industry analysts, and statisticians. It is interested in people with degrees or backgrounds in international trade, law, economics, textiles, chemistry, metallurgy, engineering, marketing, agriculture, forestry, and business administration. Applications are only accepted during periods of vacancy, which are publicized in the Washington, D.C., metropolitan area, and in the Federal Research Service publication. For more information, write to:

International Trade Commission
500 E Street, NW
Washington, DC 20436

Domestic-Oriented Agencies

The **Federal Bureau of Investigation (FBI)*** investigates criminal acts and conducts counterintelligence operations within the United States. However, the FBI also maintains legal attachés at embassies around the world. Unfortunately, it is only possible for an FBI agent to obtain one of these positions after serving several years in the FBI and overcoming very keen competition.

Special Agent Linguists, *Language Specialists*, and *Contract Linguists* are also hired by the FBI to assist in investigative work, which might include surveillance, interviewing witnesses and suspects, apprehending fugitives and criminals, collecting evidence, providing testimony in court, and other duties. Working as a *Special Agent Linguist* might require monitoring a court-authorized wiretap in a drug case, examining business records to investigate white collar crime, collecting evidence of espionage activities, blocking terrorist activity, or handling sensitive undercover assignments.

The translating work of *Language Specialists* and *Contract Linguists* is primarily document-to-document or audio-to-document. The subject matter may be in any area in which the FBI has jurisdiction, including investigations into organized crime, white collar crime, public corruption, etc.

Special Agent Linguists need a bachelor's degree in any discipline, plus fluency in a language for which the bureau has need. *Special Agent Linguists* as well as the *Language Specialists* and *Contract Linguists* must pass the FBI language tests oral tests and written translations.

At the time of publication, the FBI was experiencing a hiring freeze which was expected to last until 1994. For information, contact:

Federal Bureau of Investigation
Language Services Unit, Room 3505
J. Edgar Hoover Building
9th Street and Pennsylvania Avenue, NW
Washington, DC 20535
(202) 324-4960/3000

The **Foreign Agricultural Service (FAS)** of the Department of Agriculture is an export-promotion agency for U.S. agriculture. It improves access to foreign markets for U.S. farm products through representation to foreign governments and participation in trade negotiations. The FAS also analyzes the foreign supply and demand for agricultural products in order to forecast the potential foreign market for American agricultural products. FAS operatives worldwide with personnel located in more than 80 posts covering more than 110 countries. The overseas staff is backed up by a team of analysts, negotiators, and marketing specialists located in Washington, D.C.

Career positions in the FAS are normally filled by highly-qualified agricultural economists with master's degrees. Anyone interested in applying for a position in the FAS must file a mid-level examination with the Office of Personnel Management and send a Personal Qualifications Statement along with college transcripts to the FAS.

Selected applicants usually spend three years in Washington, D.C., in a career development program. After this period, those interested in serving abroad must compete for a position as a Foreign Service Officer, where, if successful, an officer serves as an agricultural attaché at a U.S. embassy. For information, write:

Recruitment Officer
USDA/Foreign Agricultural Service
Room 5627 South Building
14th and Independence Avenue, SW
Washington, DC 20250-1000

The **International Trade Administration (ITA)** of the Department of Commerce contains four divisions that employ individuals with backgrounds in marketing, international business, law, and economics. With the exception of Foreign Commercial Service (FCS) officers, all divisions operate in the United States and accept candidates with varying qualifications.

FCS officers identify agents and distributors for U.S. firms, locate sources of financing, and conduct market research for American firms wishing to do business abroad. They also resolve trade and investment disputes and organize trade promotion programs. FCS officers are taken from the Foreign Service and typically spend half their professional lives abroad. For information, write:

Office of Foreign Service Personnel
    and Foreign Commercial Service
Department of Commerce
Room 3815
Washington, DC 20230
(202) 482-4701

Other Agencies with International Divisions

Congressional Budget Office
Fiscal Analysis Division
2d and D Streets, SW
Washington, DC 20515
(202) 226-2621

Department of Energy
1000 Independence Avenue, SW
Forrestal Building
Washington, DC 20585
(202) 586-5000

Department of Justice
Room 5214, Main
10th and Constitution Avenue, NW
Washington, DC 20530
(202) 514-9500

Department of Labor
Bureau of International Labor Affairs
200 Constitution Avenue, NW
Washington, DC 20210
(202) 219-6666

Department of Transportation
International Affairs
400 7th Street, SW
Washington, DC 20590
(202) 366-4000

Environmental Protection Agency
International Activities, A-106
401 M Street, SW
Washington, DC 20460

Export-Import Bank of the United States
Personnel Director
811 Vermont Avenue, NW
Washington, DC 20571
(202) 566-8834

Federal Maritime Commission
800 North Capital Street, NW
Washington, DC 20573
(202) 523-5725

General Accounting Office
National Security & International Affairs
411 G Street, NW
Washington, DC 20548
(202) 275-5067

General Services, Administration
18th and F Streets, NW
Washington, DC 20405
(202) 512-3000

House Foreign Affairs Committee
RHOB, Room 2170
Washington, DC 20515
(202) 225-5021

NASA
400 Maryland Avenue, SW
Washington, DC 20546

National Science Foundation
Division of International Program
1800 G Street, NW
Washington, DC 20550

National Telecommunications and
    Information Administration (NTIA)
Chief, Management Division
Department of Commerce
NTIA/H-4890
Washington, DC 20230

Senate Foreign Relations Committee
SD-446, Dirkson Senate Office Building
Washington, DC 20510
(202) 224-4651

Resources for Federal Government Employment

Almanac of American Governments Jobs and Careers. 1991. Ron L. and Caryl R. Krannich. Impact Publications. (703) 361-7300.

Complete Guide to Public Employment. 1990. 2d ed. Ronald L. and Caryl R. Krannich. Impact Publications. (703) 361-7300.

Federal Jobs Overseas, US Office of Personnel Management, Washington, DC 20415. Brochure.

Foreign Service Officer. 1991. Jack Rudman. National Learning Corporation, 212 Michael Drive, Syosset, NY 11791. (800) 645-6337.

Guide to Careers in World Affairs. 1993. Foreign Policy Association, c/o Cup Services, PO Box 6525, Ithaca, NY 14850. (800) 477-5836.

How to Get a Federal Job. 1989. 7th ed. Rev. ed. David E. Waelde. Fedhelp Publications, 1354 Emerald Street, NE, Washington, DC 20002. (202) 397-7704

How to Get a Job Overseas. 1987. Robert Hancock and Sylvia Carpenter. Broughton Hall, 1919 State Street, Suite 112, Santa Barbara, CA 93101.

"A New Breed of Diplomat," *New York Times Magazine,* 11 Sept. 1983, 66.

"Women in the Foreign Service," *Cosmopolitan,* June 1982, 228.

Section 10
United Nations

People from a variety of backgrounds work with the United Nations and fill an equally wide variety of positions from public information officers, to translators, to secretaries. Those who work with the United Nations have challenging but rewarding careers.

Due to UN hiring practices involving a geographic quota system, Americans have a difficult time getting hired. Furthermore, the UN is committed to giving opportunities to talented individuals from developing countries. Americans with graduate degrees and experience have a better chance at higher levels and in specialized fields; generally an M.A. or Ph.D. and several years of experience are required. For professional positions, the UN generally hires highly-trained specialists with advanced degrees.

To apply for a job with the United Nations, contact the appropriate office, or write:

Office of UN Employment Information and Assistance
2201 C Street NW
Department of State
Washington, DC 20520-6323
(202) 736-4824

The **Food and Agricultural Organization of the United Nations (FAO)** seeks to improve nutrition and living standards in poor areas of the world, concentrating on rural development. FAO is the leading international body for food and agriculture, and is involved at every level of agricultural development—from demonstrating to subsistence farmers new techniques for cultivating food crops to advising governments on how to achieve more stable and equitable international trade in agricultural commodities.

An advanced degree in nutrition, economics, development, world resources, or an agriculture-related field is required for all professional positions. For information, contact:

Executive Officer
FAO Liaison Office for North America
1001 22d Street, NW, Suite 300
Washington, DC 20437
(202) 653-2400/2401

The **Secretariat** serves the Secretary General of the United Nations, who is the chief administrative officer of the whole system: the General Assembly, the Security Council, the Economic and Social Council, and the Trusteeship Council. Specialists are needed in economics, economic development, area studies, administration, agriculture, communications, and social sciences, among others. Preference is given to candidates with a knowledge of the official UN languages (English, French, Spanish, Arabic, Chinese, or Russian).

United Nations *Interpreters* must have a thorough knowledge of at least three of the UN's official languages. As a rule, they interpret into their main language and must have full auditory comprehension of at least two of the other official languages. Linguistic knowledge must cover a wide variety of fields encompassing political, economic, legal, and literary topics. Mere ability to converse socially in several languages is definitely not sufficient.

Besides linguistic knowledge and skill, a United Nations interpreter must be equipped with education and experience enough to have a thorough understanding of the various subjects debated in any of the meetings to which interpreters may be assigned—or at least the intellectual ability to acquire this understanding by study. Applicants must hold a degree from a university or an institution of equivalent status. They must also have two hundred days of experience as a conference interpreter for which they will be asked to furnish documentary proof. Candidates are also required to pass an examination to ascertain their professional skills and language proficiency. For information, contact the Office of UN Employment Information and Assistance at the above address.

The **United Nations Children's Emergency Fund (UNICEF)** is committed to promoting peace and human welfare through international development. Its mandate is to promote and support national programs to meet the special needs of children, which involves its staff in the full range of issues confronting developing societies today.

Applicants should have an advanced degree in health, nutrition, primary education, social welfare, sociology/anthropology, public administration, accounting, journalism/communications, civil engineering, or information systems; language fluency in English, French, Spanish, or Arabic; and previous field work or related work experience in a developing country. For information, contact:

Chief, Recruitment and Staff
Development Section
Division of Personnel (H-5F)
UNICEF House
3 United Nations Plaza
New York, NY 10017
(212) 326-7000

The **United Nations Conference on Trade and Development (UNCTAD)** was created as a forum of discussion for developing countries who have specific concerns to address that may otherwise not be discussed in the General Assembly. Employment is restricted to nationals of the member-nations, of which the United States is not one. Professionals must have a Ph.D. in most cases. For more information, qualified citizens of developing countries may write:

New York Liaison Office
Room S-927
United Nations
New York, NY 10017
(212) 963-6896

The **United Nations Development Program (UNDP)*** has a large network and sponsors five thousand development projects in developing countries. UNDP has three official languages (Spanish, French, English), and personnel must speak at least two. In addition, graduate degrees are required. UNDP recruits and hires internationally. For information, write:

Chief of Recruitment Section
Division of Personnel
UN Development Program
One UN Plaza
New York, NY 10017
(212) 906-5000

UN Development Program
Washington Office
1889 F Street, NW
Ground Floor
Washington, DC 20006
(202) 289-8674

The **United Nations Field Service** is a corps responsible for servicing the various UN field missions. Its personnel is subject to rotation from mission to mission in any part of the world. The Field Service is comprised of five main occupational groups: security officers, vehicle mechanics, radio technicians, radio officers, and secretaries. New staff may not normally be accompanied to their duty station by their families. For information, contact the Office of UN Employment Information and Assistance at the address given earlier.

The **United Nations Industrial Development Organization (UNIDO)*** does not require applications for specific vacancies, since applications of qualified candidates are retained in UNIDO's computerized roster, the major source of recruitment for vacancies. While a quota system is followed to maintain balance among its member-nations, UNIDO is especially committed to increasing the representation of women among its professional staff.

Expertise is required mainly in these areas: industrial engineering; specialization in industrial subsectors, e.g., chemical and mechanical engineering, metallurgical and agro-industries; economics, including econometrics; management sciences; technical assistance; project formulation and development; and administration (from personnel administration to contracting and purchasing). An advanced degree and at least two years of relevant experience are required. Prior experience in developing countries is an asset but not a necessity. Candidates must be fluent in English and French. A working knowledge of Arabic, Chinese, Russian, or Spanish is also desirable. For more information, contact:

United Nations Industrial Development Organization
1 UN Plaza
Room DC1-1110
New York, NY 10017
(212) 963-6890

United Nations Industrial Development Organization
PO Box 300
Vienna International Center
A-1400 Vienna
AUSTRIA

The **United Nations International Bank for Reconstruction and Development (IBRD)**, unofficially known as the World Bank, is a group of financial institutions formed to fund development projects in developing countries. Today the World Bank is involved in a variety of projects, from agriculture to health care to business ventures. With offices around the globe, the World Bank has opportunities for individuals with graduate degrees in economics, finance, or related fields. Previous work experience is required and language skills are preferred. Like other financial institutions, the World Bank sponsors a Young Professionals Program for candidates with a master's degree or Ph.D. For information, contact:

> Young Professionals Program
> World Bank
> 1818 H Street, NW
> Washington, DC 20433
> (202) 477-1234

The **United Nations Institute for Training and Research (UNITAR)*** trains new UN personnel but also conducts research for the Secretary General and promotes international cooperation through diplomacy. An advanced degree is necessary for professional positions; French is the preferred language. Interns must have an M.A. in international relations, political science, international law, economics, or a related field. For information, contact:

> Secretary of the UNITAR Appointment and Promotion Board
> UNITAR
> 801 UN Plaza
> New York, NY 10017
> (212) 963-8621/8622

The **World Health Organization (WHO)** works in 170 countries to provide means for all people to access health care. Among other activities, the organization conducts immunization campaigns and provides technical assistance to governments. Highly specialized professionals with advanced training and degrees are sought in health-related fields, such as doctors, researchers, and nutritionists. For information, contact:

> WHO New York Liaison Office
> UN Rooms DC2-0956-9076
> New York, NY 10017
> (212) 963-6004/6005

World Health Organization
Regional Office for the Americas
525 23d Street, NW
Washington, DC 20037
(202) 861-3200

World Health Organization
20 Avenue Appia
CH-1211 Geneva 27
SWITZERLAND

Related International Organizations

International Financial Institutions

The Office of UN Employment Information and Assistance (IO/EA) does not directly recruit for financial institutions or for some of the regional or Inter-American organizations. Candidates interested in the organizations listed below should contact the individual institution or its corresponding federal agency directly.

The **Asian Development Bank (ADB)** finances large development projects throughout Asia and the Pacific region. Unlike the International Monetary Fund (IMF), the ADB sponsors a Young Professionals Program to recruit and train top business or finance graduates who may lack international experience. All employees work in Manila. For information, write:

Head, Employment and Staff Relations
Personnel Division
Asian Development Bank
Box 789
1099 Manila
PHILIPPINES

The **Inter-American Development Bank (IDB)** is similar to the Asian Development Bank, specializing in financing various projects in Latin America and the Caribbean. It has a Young Professionals Program for qualified graduates with advanced degrees and two of four official bank languages (French, English, Portuguese, Spanish). For information, contact:

Employment and Development Division
Inter-American Development Bank
1300 New York Avenue, NW
Washington, DC 20577
(202) 623-1000

The **International Monetary Fund (IMF)** is designed to promote balanced trade and economic growth. It grants loans to help nations pay debts, finance projects, or address other economic concerns. An advanced degree (Ph.D.), and intercultural experience, particularly with developing countries, is required even at entry level. For information, contact:

Recruitment Division
International Monetary Fund
700 19th Street, NW
Washington, DC 20431
(202) 623-7000

Resources for United Nations Employment

UNIDO Newsletter, United Nations Industrial Development Organization, PO Box 300, A-1400 Vienna, AUSTRIA.

Working for the United Nations. Prepared by Transitions Abroad, TAAS Guides, PO Box 34457019, Amherst, MA 01004. ($3.00 plus $.90 postage.)

"Working for the United Nations: Mid-level Positions and Internships" by Will Cantrell, *Transitions Abroad: The Guide to Learning, Living, and Working Overseas*, vol. 15, no. 1 (July/August 1991), 30-33.

SECTION 11
UNITED STATES MILITARY

For graduates with a background in international relations and area studies, the military offers many opportunities. Students may obtain an officer's commission in the armed forces through transfer to one of the service academies early in college, by attending ROTC, or after graduation. Those interested in a career in the armed forces should contact a recruiter or ROTC representative of the service branch of their choice.

While the **U.S. Air Force** offers such traditional positions as pilots, navigators, and missile launch officers, it also employs both intelligence and public affairs officers. Intelligence officers may serve in one of the following specialties: air intelligence, signals intelligence, photo interpretation, counterintelligence, or human resources.

The work of *air intelligence officers* is similar to that of CIA analysts; they read classified documents, write reports, and conduct briefings. *Signal intelligence officers* work closely with the National Security Agency (NSA) in monitoring foreign radio and telephone communications. *Counterintelligence officers* seek to prevent secret information from falling into enemy hands, while *human resource officers* conduct debriefings.

After ten to twelve years of experience, any Air Force officer may pursue a second specialty, such as becoming an embassy air attaché or pursuing a number of other overseas opportunities.

Most new officers are selected from the Air Force Academy or ROTC cadets; however, any remaining positions are filled with college graduates who have successfully completed post-graduate Officer Training School. This last group of officers will usually be assigned to positions in technical fields.

The **U.S. Army** has most career fields open to those with a background in international affairs, including positions in military intelligence, the adjutant general corps, the staff judge advocate corps, and special forces.

Military intelligence officers serve as electronic warfare officers or counterintelligence officers; the former obtain intelligence while attached to field units or work in cooperation with the NSA in training Army personnel. The counterintelligence specialty is the smallest in military intelligence and is concerned primarily with preventing foreign intelligence services from obtaining Army secrets.

As a captain or major, an officer in the *adjutant general corps* works as an administrator. Officers in the *staff judge advocate corps* are engaged in legal work; occasionally they may even work with international law. In the *special forces*, officers train members of allied armed forces in unconventional warfare.

After eight years, an Army officer may be chosen to be a Foreign Area Officer (FAO), and specialize in various geographic regions as a commander, staff officer, attaché, advisor, or instructor. Officers with combat training are preferred.

With large troop deployments in Germany, Italy, Panama, and South Korea, the Army offers many opportunities to serve abroad. Students wishing to become Army officers should either enter the Army ROTC or attend a post-graduate Officer Candidate School (OCS). OCS graduates must serve at least eight years; two must be on active duty.

Only students with at least two years of college left are eligible for ROTC; undergraduates are eligible for scholarships, while graduate students are not (except law and medical students). All Army officers are able, at mid-career, to attend graduate school at Army expense.

The **U.S. Marine Corps** has many opportunities for those with a background in international affairs. Students may become officers in the Marines by participating in the Platoon Leader Class before their senior year of school; by attending one or two summer training sessions in Quantico, Virginia; or by attending the ten-week Officer Candidate Class (OCC) after graduation.

Following OCC, a twenty-one-week Basic School prepares an officer for Marine Corps service. Then, approximately 90 percent of Basic School graduates are assigned to the occupational field of their choice (the rest receive positions not necessarily permanent, as Marine Corps officers are expected to fill a variety of other assignments).

The positions open to Marine officers are similar to those open to Army and Air Force officers.

The **U.S. Navy** also has opportunities for internationally trained students, who are eligible for a number of positions, as described below. Unlike other service branches, the Navy will guarantee the career field of future officers before they begin Officer Candidate School (OCS) or Aviation Officers Candidate School (AOCS), and, like the Marine Corps, prospective Navy officers do not commit themselves to service in the Navy until they complete OCS or AOCS.

Navy *intelligence officers* conduct research and analysis; interpret reconnaissance photos, radar, and sonar feedback; and prepare maps, charts, tables, and graphs used in planning naval operations. They also brief senior officers. They may be involved in headquarters and major staff duty, intelligence collections, and counterintelligence.

New Navy intelligence officers are usually assigned to an aviation squadron, an aircraft carrier, or an amphibious command ship, spending the first three years after training on sea duty and another two years of sea duty later in their careers. Navy officers can expect to be separated from their families about six months out of eighteen while on sea duty. Intelligence officers can also serve later in their careers as naval attachés in embassies abroad.

Surface warfare officers work in administration, maintenance, personal counseling, logistics, and other support functions. *Flight officers* are responsible for weapons control, electronic detection and countermeasures, and some intelligence gathering. *Cryptological officers* do work similar to that done by the NSA. Officers in the Supply Corps supply everything except weaponry; they also work in budgeting, cost control, purchasing, and inventory management and distribution. *Supply officers* specialize in financial management, inventory management, or food service management.

All Navy officers are eligible for advance training and postgraduate schooling. The time commitment to the Navy varies with the different occupational fields.

SECTION 12
NONPROFIT ORGANIZATIONS

Nonprofit organizations are part of a fast-growing sector referred to as non-government organizations (NGOs). Most are supported by private donations; some receive grants to operate; others sell publications to cover operating costs.

Both nonprofit and volunteer organizations use volunteers. Both offer salaried positions as well; although, the pay is usually less than in the private sector. For this reason, NGO professionals must be committed to the cause of the organization. They are, after all, service oriented, which keeps salaries down. Although salaries are moderate, these positions are competitive. Former interns are frequently hired when these salaried positions are available.

The selected organizations below offer only a sampling of the many organizations operating worldwide. For a more comprehensive review of possibilities, refer to the more specialized publications listed under Additional Resources, which again, provide only a place to begin.

Assistance, Relief, and Development Organizations

Cooperative for American Relief Everywhere (CARE)* hires a limited number of international staff employees based on their technical knowledge in such areas as agriculture, economic development, health care, nutrition, project management, and engineering. Positions are competitive. Potential candidates should also have prior experience working in developing countries and second language proficiency. Interested, qualified candidates should send resume and cover letter to:

International Employment CARE
151 Ellis Street
Atlanta, GA 30303

The **Tolstoy Foundation, Inc.,** is a refugee assistance organization designed to help political dissidents and immigrants enter the United States and to assist them during resettlement. It also operates several residence homes for elderly people. A degree in social service or other relevant field is preferred and language skills are required, (especially for languages used most by immigrants from Central Europe, Asia, and Latin America). For information, contact:

Executive Director
Tolstoy Foundation
200 Park Avenue South
New York, NY 10003
(212) 677-7770

World Vision International (WVI) is a Christian organization dedicated to relief and development. It engages in over three thousand
projects worldwide—some short-term (emergency relief) and others on
a larger scale. Employment opportunities exist in numerous fields.
Applicants need a graduate degree in business, communications, education, engineering, finance or related fields, personnel administration,
public health or a medical field, relief and rehabilitation, or technical
writing, to name only a few areas. Overseas experience in a developing
country is essential. Language fluency in Portuguese, French, or Spanish is required; a willingness to learn Khmer is necessary in some cases.
Computer skills are helpful. For information, contact:

Employment Manager
World Vision International
919 West Huntington Drive
Monrovia, CA 91016
(818) 303-8811

Educational and Cultural Exchange Organizations

The **American Field Service (AFS)*** hires internally, so an internship
can provide entrance into AFS. Most positions will be filled by recent
college graduates with a bachelor's degrees in communications, journalism, English, or area studies, with intercultural knowledge and
experience, knowledge of AFS programs, and experience in a related
field. For information, contact:

AFS Intercultural Programs
220 E 42d Street 3d Floor
New York, NY 10017-5806
(212) 949-4242

The **International Management and Development Institute (IMDI)**
works to promote international cooperation and better understanding
between governments and private sector interests. As an educational
institute, it sponsors seminars, research projects, and publications.
Entry level employees perform a support role. For information, contact:

IMDI
2600 Virginia Avenue, NW, Suite 1112
Washington, DC 20037
(202) 337-1022

Youth for Understanding (YFU)* offers staff positions for individuals with degrees in international affairs or related fields. An internship would be advantageous. For more information, contact:

Assistant Director, Volunteer Services
Youth for Understanding
Newark Street, NW
Washington, DC 22016
(202) 966-6800

Research Institutions

The American Enterprise Institute for Public Policy Research (AEI)* has a division for international affairs and publishes scholarly and other research materials covering a wide range of topics. Positions are available for candidates with M.A. or Ph.D. degrees. For information, contact:

American Enterprise Institute for Public Policy Research
17th Street, NW
Washington, DC 20036
(202) 862-5800

The **Brookings Institute** researches issues of public policy. One division conducts foreign policy research; the other two divisions work with government studies and economic studies. The Institute also sponsors lectures and publications. Candidates must have foreign language skills and at least a master's degree to obtain entry-level research positions. For information, contact:

Brookings Institute
1775 Massachusetts Avenue, NW
Washington, DC 20036
(202) 797-6000

Note: For resources on volunteer and nonprofit organizations, see page 62.

Teaching and Education Organizations

To teach in public schools in the United States, a current teaching certificate is required in most states, along with a degree representative of the level being taught (B.A. for elementary and secondary; M.A. and Ph.D. for higher education). A minor is also encouraged for greater expertise and versatility. Requirements differ for private schools. Contact your university's education department for information relating to current state and local requirements.

Teaching abroad is not only potentially rewarding but challenging as well. Competition for positions locally as well as abroad is often keen, but numerous opportunities are available to qualified candidates, who are usually required to have at least one or two years of professional experience.

Generally, positions abroad are not permanent but are based on short-term contracts. An interested individual would be wise to make arrangements for continued or alternate employment when the contract has expired. One of the safest ways to do so is through teacher exchanges, where teachers switch places for one year. The Department of Education sponsors an exchange program for teachers with master's degrees in Teaching English as a Foreign Language/Teaching English as a Second Language (TEFL/TESL) or a closely related field. For information, contact:

US Information Agency
English Teaching Fellow Program (E/CE)
Room 304, 301 4th Street, SW
Washington, DC 20547
(202) 619-5869

Opportunities are also available in schools operated by American businesses and Department of Defense schools, which operate schools in twenty countries and recruits over five hundred teachers each year. Teachers hired are given a one or two-year assignment in a country where they are needed—not necessarily in a nation of their choice. Information is available from:

US Department of Defense
Office of Overseas Dependents Schools
Teacher Recruitment Section
2461 Eisenhower Avenue
Hoffman Building #1, Room 112
Alexandria, VA 22331-1100
(703) 696-3068

For a list of State Department-assisted schools, contact:

Director of the Office of Overseas Schools (A/OS)
Room 245, SA-29
Department of State
Washington, DC 20522-2902
(703) 875-7800

Many organizations and school systems recruit and employ U.S. citizens for teaching positions in foreign countries, U.S. territories, and outlying states. The organizations listed below can provide information about opportunities to teach abroad at the elementary, secondary, and postsecondary levels. Please contact these agencies directly if you wish to receive information about their programs. Many countries recruit educators through their embassies in Washington, D.C. If you wish to teach in a specific country, you may find it valuable to contact the educational officer of the foreign embassy.

AFS International Intercultural Programs
220 E 42d Street
New York, NY 10017
(212) 949-4242
Eight-week exchanges with Russia, Latin America, and East Asia.

British American Educational Foundation
PO Box 33
Larchmont, NY 10538
(212) 340-8901
Clearinghouse for independent school exchanges.
For more information, contact Charles at (401) 727-2438.

Council for International Exchange of Scholars (CIES)
3007 Tilden Street, NW, Suite 5M
Washington, DC 20008-3009
(202) 686-4000

Center for International Education
US Department of Education
400 Maryland Avenue, SW
Washington, DC 20202-5247
(202) 732-6061

English Teaching Fellowship Program
English Language Programs Division
United States Information Agency
301 4th Street, SW, E/CE, Room 304
Washington, DC 20547
(202) 619-5869

European Council of International Schools
21B Lavant Street
Petersfield, Hampshire
GU32 3EL
ENGLAND

Faculty Exchange Center
952 Virginia Avenue
Lancaster, PA 17603
(717) 393-1130

The International Educator
PO Box 513
Kummaquid, MA 02637
(508) 362-1414

International Schools Services, Inc.
15 Roszel Road PO Box 5910
Princeton, NJ 08543
(609) 452-0990

National Association of Foreign Students Affairs
Association of International Educators
Department of Education
1875 Connecticut Avenue, NW, Suite 1000
Washington, DC 20009
(202) 462-4811

National Faculty Exchange
4656 West Jefferson, Suite 140
Fort Wayne, IN 46804
(219) 436-2634

Various networking organizations exist for individuals who are interested in specific areas. The list below is not meant to be comprehensive; it is only offered as a sampling of possibilities.

Area Studies
Association of Teachers of Latin American Studies
6505 Alvorado Road, Suite 205
San Diego, CA 92120-5011

Committee on Atlantic Studies
c/o Robert J. Jackson
Carleton University
Department of Political Science
Ottawa Ontario
1125 Colonel By Drive, Loeb Building B640
CANADA K1S 5B6
(613) 788-2780

Business
International Association of Business Communicators
1 Hallidie Plaza, Suite 600
San Francisco, CA 94102
(415) 433-3400

History
International Committee for Historical Sciences
13, rue Jacob
F-75006 Paris
FRANCE

Intercultural Relations
Institute for Cultural Studies
165 East 72th Street, Suite 1B
New York, NY 10021
(212) 737-1011

Intercultural Communication Institute
8835 SW Canyon Lane, Suite 238
Portland, OR 97225
(503) 297-4622

SIETAR International
1505 22d Street, NW
Washington, DC 20037
(202) 296-4710

International Relations
International Studies Association
David M. Kennedy Center for International Studies
216 HRCB
Brigham Young University
Provo, UT 84602
(801) 378-5459

Languages
American Association of Teachers of Arabic
David M. Kennedy Center for International Studies
280 HRCB
Brigham Young University
Provo, UT 84602

American Association of Teachers of French
57 East Armory Avenue
Champaign, IL 61820
(217) 333-2842
American Association of Teachers of German
112 Haddontowne Court #104
Cherry Hill, NJ 08034-3662
(609) 795-5553

American Association of Teachers of Italian
c/o Albert N. Mancini
Chicago State University
Department of French and Italian
Columbus, OH 43210
(614) 292-2273

American Association of Teachers of Spanish and Portuguese
c/o Lynn Sandstedt
University of Northern Colorado
Greeley, CO 80639

Political Science
American Academy of Political and Social Science
3937 Chestnut Street
Philadelphia, PA 19104
(215) 386-4594

American Political Science Association (APSA)
1527 New Hampshire Avenue, NW
Washington, DC 20036
(202) 483-2512

Resources on Teaching and Education

Directories

ISS Directory of Overseas Schools. 12th ed. 1992. International Schools Services, Inc., 15 Roszel Road, PO Box 5910, Princeton, NJ 08540. (800) 338-3282. Distributed by Peterson's Guides.

Newsletters

International Education Placement Hotline, PDRC Placement Hotline, c/o PDRC, F-6, School for International Living, Kipling Road, PO Box 676, Brattleboro, VT 05302-0676. ($25 yr./12 issues).

Publications

Educators' Passport to International Jobs: How to Find & Enjoy Employment Abroad. 1984. Rebecca Anthony and Gerald Roe. Published by Peterson's Guides. (800) EDU-DATA.

International Jobs—Where They Are, How to Get Them: A Handbook for Over 500 Career Opportunities. 1989. 3d ed., rev. Eric Kocher. Addison-Wesley Publishing. Reading, MA.

Peterson's Guide to Independent Secondary Schools. Peterson's Guides. (800) EDU-DATA.

Schools Abroad of Interest to Americans. 8th ed. 1991. Porter Sargent Staff Publications, Inc., 11 Beacon Street, Suite 1400, Boston, MA 02108. (617) 523-1670.

Teaching Abroad. 1988–91. 1988. Edited by B. C. Connotillo, Institute of International Education (IIE). Distributed by Peterson's Guides. (800) EDU-DATA.

SECTION 13
GENERAL RESOURCES FOR THE INTERNATIONALLY MINDED INDIVIDUAL

Associations, Publishers, and Organizations

Council on International Education Exchange (CIEE) 205 East 42d Street, New York, NY 10017. (212) 661-1414.

Impact Publications, 9104-N Manassas Drive, Manassas Park, VA 22111-5211. (703) 361-7300. Publishes materials on career-finding and the international market. Write or call for a free publications catalog.

Intercultural Press, PO Box 700, Yarmouth, ME 04096. (207) 846-5168.

Institute of International Education, 809 UN Plaza, New York, NY 10017-3580. (212) 883-8200. IIE Publications. (212) 984-5412.

Peterson's Guides, 202 Carnagie Center, PO Box 2123, Princeton, NJ 08543-2123. (800) EDU-DATA.

World Trade Academy Press, Inc., 50 East 42d Street, Suite 509, New York, NY 10017. (212) 697-4999. Ask for a catalog.

WorldWise Books, PO Box 3030, Oakton, VA 22124. (703) 620-1972. Ask for a catalog.

Directories

Directory of American Firms Operating in Foreign Countries. 1992. (3 vols.) World Trade Academy Press.

Directory of Foreign Firms Operating in the United States. 1992. World Trade Academy Press.

Yearbook of International Organizations 1988-89, Union of International Associations, 1988.

Newsletters

Career Opportunities News, Garrett Park Press PO Box 190, Garrett Park, MD 20896. (301) 946-2553. ($25 yr./6 issues.)

Career World General Learning Corp, 3500 Western Avenue, Highland Park, IL 60035. ($4.95 yr./9 issues.)

Community Jobs: The Employment Newspaper for the Nonprofit Sector. Access: Networking in the Public Interest, 50 Beacon Street, Boston, MA 02108. (617) 720-5627. ($39/6 issues or $29/3 issues.)

International Affairs Career Bulletin. Jeffries & Associates, Inc., 17200 Hughes Road, Poolesville, MD 20837. (301) 972-8034. ($95/12 issues.)

International Employment Opportunities, Route 2, Box 305, Standardsville, VA 22973. (804) 985-6444. ($129 yr./ 26 issues.) This publication also produces *International Professionals Available*— for applicants who send in ads. *International Employment Opportunities* lists current openings in the United States and abroad, in foreign affairs, international trade and finance, international development and assistance, foreign languages, international program administration, and international education and exchange programs with the federal government, U.S. corporations, nonprofit and international institutions.

International Employment Gazette. 1525 Wade Hampton Boulevard, Greenville, SC 29609. (800) 882-9188. ($35/3 mo. subscription or 6 issues.) Biweekly newsletter listing 400+ job openings around the world in all occupations.

International Employment Hotline, Box 3030, Oakton, VA 22124. ($36 yr./12 issues.) Monthly newsletter giving names and addresses for international employers in government, nonprofit organizations, and private companies.

International Employment Hotline, PO Box 6170, McLean, VA 22106. ($26 yr./12 issues.)

State (newsletter for the U.S. Department of State—also available to public), Superintendent of Documents, US Government Printing Office, Washington, DC 20402.

Transitions Abroad, Department TRA, PO Box 3000, Denville, NJ 07834. (800) 562-1973. ($18/6 issues.) (For back issues, contact *Transitions Abroad*, 18 Hulst Road, PO Box 1300, Amherst, MA 01004. (413) 256-0373.

Publications

The Almanac of International Jobs and Careers. 1991. Ron L. & Caryl R. Krannich. Impact Publications. (703) 361-7300.

Careers and the Study of Political Science: A Guide for Undergraduates. 1985. Mary H. Curzan. American Political Science Association, 1527 New Hampshire Avenue, NW, Washington, DC 20036. (202) 483-2512.

Careers for People Who Love to Travel. 1986. Joy Mullett and Lois Darley. Prentice-Hall, 15 Columbus Circle, New York, NY 10023. (800) 223-2348.

The Complete Guide to International Jobs and Careers. 1992. Ronald L. and Caryl R. Krannich. Impact Publications. (703) 361-7300.

Encyclopedia of Careers and Vocational Guidance. 1990. 4 vols. Ed. William Hopke. J. G. Ferguson Publishing, 200 West Madison Street, Suite 300, Chicago, IL 60606. (312) 580-5480.

International Jobs—Where They Are, How to Get Them: A Handbook for Over 500 Career Opportunities (3d ed., rev.) 1989. Eric Kocher. Reading, MA, Addison-Wesley Publishing. (800) 447-2226

Jobs for People Who Love Travel. 1993. Ron L. and Caryl R. Krannich. Impact Publications. (703) 361-7300.

Looking for Employment in Foreign Countries. 1992. 9th ed. World Trade Academy Press. (212) 697-4999.

Making It Abroad: The International Job Hunting Guide. 1988. Howard Schuman. John Wiley & Sons, 605 Third Avenue, New York, NY 10158-0012.

Moving Your Family Overseas. 1992. Rosalind C. Kalb and Penelope A. Welch. Intercultural Press. (207) 846-5168.

The Occupational Outlook Handbook. 1990-91 ed. Washington, DC: US Department of Labor, Bureau of Labor Statistics Staff. Associated Book Publishers, PO Box 5657, 12004 North Falcon Drive, Scottsdale, AZ 85261-5657. (602) 837-9388.

The Overseas List: Opportunities for Living and Working in Developing Countries. 1985. David M. Beckmann, Timothy J. Mitchell, and Linda L. Powers. Minneapolis: Augsburg Fortress. 57 East Main Street, Columbus, OH 43215-5183. (800) 848-2738.

Survival Kit for Overseas Living—For Americans Planning to Live and Work Abroad. 1984. L. Robert Kohls. Intercultural Press. (207) 846-5168.

What Color is Your Parachute? A Practical Manual for Job-Hunters and Career Changers. 1993. Richard Bolles. Berkeley, CA: Ten Speed Press. (800) 841-2665.

Work Your Way Around the World. 1989. Susan Griffith. Peterson's Guides. (800) EDU-DATA.

Appendix

Programs for BYU Students

Appendix
Programs for BYU Students

Washington Seminar is primarily an academic internship program designed to provide students with the opportunity to work in a professional setting while studying the current issues of the day. Juniors, seniors, and graduate students of all academic majors with a minimum grade point average of 3.0 on a 4.0 scale are invited to apply. For information, contact:

Washington Seminar
Brigham Young University
745 SWKT
Provo, UT 84602
(801) 378-6029

Washington Seminar Faculty Residence
6066 Morgan Court
Alexandria, VA 22312
(703) 354-9131

The **Cooperative Education Office** works with students and employers to create positive work experiences for students. In addition, most colleges and departments have cooperative education coordinators. For information on the opportunities and benefits of this academic area, contact:

Cooperative Education Office
Brigham Young University
110 FOB
Provo, UT 84602
(801) 378-3337

BYU Travel Study combines academic, spiritual, and intercultural goals and is especially designed for people who enjoy traveling with those who share their standards and are willing to abide by those standards. Since the early 1950s, BYU Travel Study has taken thousands of people to the Middle East, Central and South America, Europe, the Orient, the South Pacific, and other areas of the world. University credit is available to those who wish to complete assignments related to travel experiences. For information, contact:

Travel Study
Brigham Young University
309 HCEB
Provo, UT 84602
(801) 378-3946

Asia - Pacific Institute of Studies

BYU Study Abroad offers programs in Italy, London, Madrid, Mexico, Paris, the People's Republic of China, and Vienna for fall/winter semesters or spring/summer terms. In some instances students may live with native families so as to be exposed to local foods, values, and customs. Courses offered meet general education requirements for some majors and feature learning experiences designed to involve students personally and actively with the people and their history, arts, attitudes, and traditions. For information, contact:

Study Abroad
Brigham Young University
204 HRCB
Provo, UT 84602
(801) 378-3308

The **International Internship Program** is designed to assist students in locating and tailoring an internship that fits their academic objectives and for which they can receive university credit. Students have been placed in Germany, Japan, Mexico, Spain, Taiwan, and many other countries in organizations related to their respective areas of study. These have included advertising, audiology, biology, business, clothing and textiles, communications, rural development, marketing, and sports administration.

Although the International Internship Office will guide and assist students in developing the right sponsor, students take the responsibility for initiating and planning international internships. For information, contact:

International Internship Program
Brigham Young University
204-D HRCB
Provo, UT 84602
(801) 378-6192